DAVID EDGAR

David Edgar was born in 1948 into a theatre family. After a period in journalism, he took up writing full time in 1972. In 1989, he founded Britain's first graduate playwriting course, at the University of Birmingham, of which he was director for ten years. He was appointed as Britain's first Professor of Playwriting in 1995.

His original stage plays include *Death Story* (Birmingham Repertory Theatre, 1972), *Entertaining Strangers* (Dorchester Community Play, 1985, then National Theatre 1987), *That Summer* (Hampstead Theatre, London, 1987) and *The Shape of the Table* (National Theatre 1990). His stage adaptations include Albie Sachs's *Jail Diary* (Royal Shakespeare Company, 1978), Mary Barnes and Joe Berke's *Mary Barnes* (Birmingham Rep then Royal Court, London, 1978-9), a multi-award-winning version of Dickens's *Nicholas Nickleby* (Royal Shakespeare Company in London and New York, 1980-1, subsequently Channel 4), Stevenson's *Dr Jekyll and Mr Hyde* (Royal Shakespeare Company, 1991 and then Birmingham Rep, 1996) and Gitta Sereny's *Albert Speer* (National Theatre, 2000). His original plays for the RSC are *Destiny* (1976), *Maydays* (1983) and *Pentecost* (1994-5), which won, respectively, the John Whiting Award, the *Plays and Players* play of the year award, and the *Evening Standard* best play award.

David Edgar's television work includes the three-part serial *Vote for Them* (written with Neil Grant, BBC2, 1989), the single play *Buying a Landslide* (BBC2, 1992) and *Citizen Locke* (Channel Four, 1994). His radio work for the BBC includes *Talking to Mars* (1996) and and an adaptation of Eve Brook's novel *The Secret Parts* (2000). He also wrote the film *Lady Jane* for Paramount (1986). He writes and reviews for a wide variety of journals, including the *Guardian*, the *New Statesman* and the *London Review of Books*. He has published a volume of essays (*The Second Time as Farce*, 1988), and he edited and introduced a book on contemporary playwriting, *State of Play*, published in 1999.

Also by David Edgar

Albert Speer

Destiny

Dr Jekyll and Mr Hyde

Entertaining Strangers

The Jail Diary of Albie Sachs

Mary Barnes

Nicholas Nickleby

Pentecost

Teendreams & Our Own People

That Summer

The Shape of the Table

Wreckers

Vote for Them

Edgar Plays: One (*Destiny, Mary Barnes, The Jail Diary of Albie Sachs, Saigon Rose, O Fair Jerusalem*)

Edgar Plays: Two (*Ecclesiastes, Nicholas Nickleby, Entertaining Strangers*)

Edgar Plays: Three (*Our Own People, Teendreams, Maydays, That Summer*)

Edgar: Shorts (*Blood Sports* with *Ball Boys, Baby Love, The National Theatre, The Midas Connection*)

The Second Time as Farce

State of Play (*editor and introduction*)

David Edgar

THE PRISONER'S DILEMMA

NICK HERN BOOKS
London
www.nickhernbooks.co.uk

A Nick Hern Book

The Prisoner's Dilemma first published in this revised edition
in 2002 as an original paperback by Nick Hern Books Limited,
14 Larden Road, London W3 7ST, in association with the
Royal Shakespeare Company, Barbican Centre, London EC2Y 8BQ

Reprinted 2003

The Prisoner's Dilemma © 2001, 2002 by David Edgar

Afterword © 2002 by David Edgar

David Edgar has asserted his right to be identified as
the author of this work

Typeset by Country Setting, Kingsdown, Kent CT14 8ES
Printed in Great Britain by Bookmarque, Croydon, Surrey

A CIP catalogue record for this book is available from
the British Library

ISBN 185459 679 9

To Clarissa Brown

Acknowledgements

I am obligated to Helen Rappaport, Kevin Smith and Tiia Tempakka who translated and taught the languages used in the play.

For research help I am grateful to Lawrence Freedman of King's College, London; Scilla Elworthy of the Oxford Research Group; Hugh Miall of the University of Lancaster; Peter Paul van der Groote of Médecin sans Frontières; and the staff and graduate students of the University of Bradford's Department of Peace Studies (including Nick Lewer, Sarah Perrigo, Tom Woodhouse, Oliver Ramsbotham, Donna Parkhurst, Tamara Duffey, Pia Johannson and Barbara Weber). For further help and advice I am grateful to Penny Cherns, Stephanie Dale, Charlotte Keatley, Ted Braun, Clarissa Brown, Esther Richardson, Hilary Norrish, Kaite O'Reilly, Levan Khetaguri, and David Sakvarelidze.

I owe a particular debt to David Kennedy of the Harvard Law School, who introduced me to the function and practice of role-play in international diplomacy (and much else besides); and to Nigel Howard, whose concept of drama-theory was crucial to the structuring of the play.

Much of the first act of *The Prisoner's Dilemma* began life as a libretto written for the Stephen Oliver award. Titled *The Bridge*, the opera was set by Tim Benjamin and presented at the Royal Northern College of Music and the Covent Garden Festival in 1998.

Finally, the quotations before and after the acts of the play are drawn from Shakespeare, various television and press reports, and the following books: *Contemporary Conflict Resolution* (Hugh Miall, Oliver Ramsbotham, Tom Woodhouse, 1999), *The Clash of Civilizations and the Remaking of World Order* (Samuel P. Huntington, 1996), *Getting to Yes* (Roger Fisher and William Ury, 1981), *Games, Threats and Treaties*

(Jon Hovi, 1998), *The Fight for Peace* (Eamonn Mallie and David McKittrick, 1996), *Gaza First* (Jane Corbin, 1994) and *Chechnya: Calamity in the Caucasus* (Carlotta Gall and Thomas de Waal, 1998).

Author's Notes

Notation

A dash (–) means that a character is interrupted. A slash (/) means that the next character to speak starts speaking at that point (what follows the slash need not be completed, it is there to indicate the character's train of thought). Ellipses (. . .) indicate that a character has interrupted him or herself.

Language

All characters speak the languages they know, whether their own or indeed English. For information, I have identified the languages and given English translations of the non-English speeches (printed in square brackets and obviously not intended to be spoken).

In this text, the non-Roman script languages are phonetically transliterated. The Kavkhaz language is in fact Bulgarian, and the Drozhdani language is largely based on Azerbaijani but contains features of other Western Turkic languages. In fact, however, neither Kavkhazia nor Drozhdania are based directly on any real country.

The transliteration is intended to render the languages in a form that will be accessible to actors, to convey the equivalent sounds of the letters, rather than their correct orthography.

In the case of the Drozhdani speeches, there are a number of vowels and consonants which have no direct equivalent in English: 'aa' is long (as in *far*); 'ö' is like the vowel in *third*, 'ü' is like the *tu* in French, and the vowel 'ı' is like the 'er' in 'father'; 'kh' is like the 'ch' in *loch*, 'gh' like the French 'r' in *Paris*, 'q' is similar to a hard C.

The play is written for fourteen actors. The doubling pattern for the first production was as follows:

Al Bek/Young Man

Floss

James/2nd Drozhdan/2nd Paramilitary

Patterson/Len

Gina/Mother

Tom/Father

Nikolai/Lou

Waiter/1st Drozhdan/2nd Orderly/Trevelyan/
    Bodyguard/Zelim/lst Paramilitary

Kelima

Jan/Boy/Aslan

Erik/Yuri Vasilevich Petrovian

Roman/2nd Kavkhazian Soldier

Hasim/1st Kavkhazian Soldier

lst Orderly/Sailor/Emela

The text published here was used for the London run of The Prisoner's Dilemma *from January 2002.*

The Prisoner's Dilemma was first performed by the Royal
Shakespeare Company at The Other Place, Stratford-upon-
Avon, on 11 July 2001. The cast was as follows:

AL BEK/YOUNG MAN	Douglas Rao
FLOSS	Diana Kent
JAMES/2ND DROZHDAN/2ND PARAMILITARY	
	David Wilmot
PATTERSON/LEN	Joseph Mydell
GINA/MOTHER	Penny Downie
TOM/FATHER	Larry Lamb
NIKOLAI/LOU	Trevor Cooper
WAITER/1ST DROZHDAN/2ND ORDERLY/	
TREVELYAN/BODYGUARD/ZELIM/	
1ST PARAMILITARY	Alex Zorbas
KELIMA	Zoe Waites
JAN/BOY/ASLAN	George Clarke/Joshua Dale
ERIK/YURI VASILEVICH	Alan David
ROMAN/2ND KAVKHAZIAN SOLDIER	Robert Bowman
HASIM/1ST KAVKHAZIAN SOLDIER	Robert Jezek
EMELA/1ST ORDERLY/SAILOR/TRANSLATOR	
	Hattie Morahan

Directed by Michael Attenborough
Designed by Es Devlin
Lighting designed by Howard Harrison
Music by Paddy Cunneen
Fights by Terry King
Sound designed by John A. Leonard for Aura
Computer Animation by Gary Vernon
Assistant Director Samantha Potter
Translators and Foreign Language Advisors
   Helen Rappaport, Kevin Smith and Tiia Tempakka
Dialect Coach Charmian Hoare
Company voice work by Andrew Wade and Charmian Hoare
Production Manager Mark Graham
Costume Supervisor Fizz Jones

xii

Scenes

Act One

One: Santa Cruz, California, early 1989

Two: Kavkhazia, eight years later

Three: Finland, two months later

Four: The same, two days later

Five: The same, the next day

Six: Geneva, three months later

Act Two

One: Kavkhazia, two years later

Two: Eastern Mediterranean, four months later

Three: The same, the next day

Four: The same, continuous

Five: Drozhdania, two years later

Characters

JAMES NEIL, *Irish, b. 1962*
FLOSS WEATHERBY, *British, b.1950*
AL BEK, *American, b.1962*
PATTERSON DAVIS, *American, b.1961*
GINA OLSSON, *Finnish, b.1956*
TOM ROTHMAN, *American, b.1942*
NIKOLAI SHUBKIN, *Kavkhazian, b.1947*
WAITER, *Afghan origin, b.1964*
1st DROZHDAN, *20s*
KELIMA BEJTA, Drozhdani, *b.1968*
2nd DROZHDAN, *mid 30s*
JAN OLSSON-TRÄSK, *Finnish, 12*
ERIK TRÄSK, *Finnish, 45*
ROMAN LITVINYENKO, *Kavkhazian b.1960*
HASIM MAJDANI, *Drozhdani, b.1945*
1st ORDERLY, *Swiss*
2nd ORDERLY, *Swiss*
TREVELYAN, *British, 33*
EMELA, *Drozhdani, 24*
LEN, *British, 30s*
1st KAVKHAZIAN SOLDIER, *30s*
2nd KAVKHAZIAN SOLDIER, *40s*
FATHER, *47*
MOTHER, *35*
YOUNG MAN, *20*
BOY, *10*
SAILOR, *American, female*
YURI VASILEVICH PETROVIAN, *Kavkhazian President, 52*
BODYGUARD, *Kavkhazian, 20s*
ZELIM ZAGAYEV, *Drozdhani, 31*
LOU WASSERMAN, *American, 52*
ASLAN, *Drozhdani, 12*
1st PARAMILITARY, *Afghan origin, 38*
2nd PARAMILITARY, *Drozhdani, 20s*

THE PRISONER'S DILEMMA

'The question "Why?" has two quite different meanings.
One looks backward for a cause and treats our behaviour
as determined by prior events. The other looks forward
for a purpose and treats our behaviour as subject
to our free will.'

Roger Fisher and William Ury
Getting to Yes, 1981

'The way to avoid the dangers of history-poisoning
or history-addiction is to regard history not as
a heap of facts, a mountain of oppressive memories,
but as a fertile field of inquiry and interpretations,
thus using the past as building material for the future.'

Amos Oz, 1992

'Why do we kill children? Because someday
they will grow up and we will have to kill them then.'

Serb Soldier, 1992

ACT ONE

'Traditionally, the task of conflict resolution
has been seen as helping parties who perceive
their situation as zero-sum (Self's gain is other's loss)
to reperceive it as a non-zero-sum conflict (in which both
may gain or both may lose) and then to assist parties
to move in the positive-sum direction.'

Miall, Ramsbotham and Woodhouse
Contemporary Conflict Resolution, 1999

'A peace is of the nature of a conquest,
For then both parties nobly are subdued,
And neither party loser.'

Shakespeare
Henry IV Part 2

'The British Government agree that it is for the people of the island of Ireland alone, by agreement between the two parts respectively, to exercise their right of self-determination on the basis of consent, freely and concurrently given, North and South, to bring about a united Ireland, if that is their wish.'

The Downing Street Declaration,
15 December 1993

'Sinn Fein has one advantage over other parties. We've brought a camp bed. We don't share it, of course.'

Gerry Adams, April 1998

'Arafat wanted the statement to read "We recognise the right of Israel to live in secure and recognized boundaries", but now agreed to change the phrase "live in secure and recognized boundaries" to "exist in peace and security".'

Jane Corbin on the Oslo negotiations

'Is the handshaking an event, or is it a gesture?'

Shimon Peres, 1993

ACT ONE

Scene One

Early 1989. An anonymous meeting room, in a Californian university. A large table, at which JAMES NEIL, *an Irish* MAN *in his late 20s and* FLOSS WEATHERBY, *a British* WOMAN *in her late 30s are sitting on one side, opposite* PATTERSON DAVIS, *a black American in his late 20s,* GINA OLSSON, *a woman of 32, with a slight Scandinavian accent, and* AL BEK, *a white American man in his mid 20s, wearing a brightly coloured short-sleeved shirt.*

AL. OK. Let's run this through again.

FLOSS. Go on.

PATTERSON. We are here to make our position absolutely clear to you.

FLOSS. As are we. You have read our statement of non-negotiable demands?

AL. Of course.

FLOSS. Comrade.

FLOSS *nods to* JAMES, *who reads:*

JAMES. They include: an immediate end to martial law, withdrawal of government troops from the areas of the indigenous peoples, the immediate release of all / political prisoners –

PATTERSON. Yes, we've read the statement.

FLOSS. And recognition of the PFLO as the acknowledged representative / of the people –

PATTERSON. As you will know on our part that there is no question of a return to normal until your campaign of violence is ceased completely. And I stop having to write letters to the widows of policemen murdered by you terrorists.

Pause.

JAMES. I don't think we're actually asking for a return to normal.

PATTERSON. No? I thought you wanted / an end to martial law –

FLOSS. Not 'normal' as in the selling off of our ancestral lands to the American imperialists. Not 'normal' as in the vicious exploitation of the workers in the cobalt mines. Which should be theirs by right.

JAMES (*consulting a paper*). Chromium.

FLOSS. I'm sorry?

JAMES. The mines are chromium.

AL. Well of course we have the right to sell rights to exploit our national resources to anyone we like. We are the government.

FLOSS. Hm!

AL *glances at* GINA, *hoping she'll come in. She doesn't, so he carries on:*

AL. But I must tell you, that since last year's wave of strikes, and now your threat to bomb the mines, not to mention your campaign of taking foreign hostages, the likelihood of investment in the mining industry is pretty limited. By American imperialists or anybody else.

JAMES. Particularly given that United Nations resolution –

PATTERSON (*under* JAMES's *speech*). Well, you know . . .

JAMES (*simultaneous*). – of last summer declaring the government to be illegitimate.

PATTERSON. Well, you know my attitude to UN resolutions!

FLOSS. Which it would be simplicity itself to have withdrawn.

PATTERSON. Oh how?

FLOSS. Stop arresting workers for asserting basic human rights.

JAMES. Get your soldiers off our streets.

AL. We'd be delighted to. Just as soon as you stop taking innocent civilians hostage.

JAMES. Which can happen just as soon as you release all members of the people's army.

PATTERSON. No problem. Just as soon as you declare an unconditional cessation of your terrorist campaign.

FLOSS. You say 'cessation'. I hear 'surrender'.

AL. You say 'people's army', I hear 'terrorist conspiracy'.

PATTERSON. A conspiracy they want us to legalise!

GINA *has been looking in her papers.*

GINA. In fact, they don't want to be legalised. Which would obviously involve accepting the government's authority. What they want is to be treated as the legitimate representative of the tribal peoples.

Slight pause.

Sounds pretty mild to me.

JAMES. Uh – does that help?

GINA. I merely make this point.

FLOSS. I'm sorry, aren't we going round in circles here?

A 47-year-old American professor, TOM ROTHMAN, *emerges from the audience.*

TOM. Well, you could say that we've reached an impasse.

JAMES *stretches back in his chair.*

JAMES (*mock Irish*). 'Thanks be to Jayzus'.

TOM. And as everybody put their case impeccably, I wonder how that happened?

Slight pause.

AL. The bastards wouldn't budge.

FLOSS. Well, we kept to our positions in the briefing book.

JAMES. Implacably.

TOM. Yes, so you did. OK. Has anybody seen the James Dean movie *Rebel without a Cause*?

Very slight pause.

AL. Yes, Professor, I have seen the movie.

TOM. Do you remember how it ends?

AL. Well, as I recall . . . two guys decide to drive two cars extremely fast straight at each other. And the one who swerves first loses.

TOM. In the sense of losing face. Miss Weatherby, you're driver A. Mr Davis here is Driver B. Run through your options.

FLOSS. Well, to swerve or not to, I suppose.

TOM. And if you swerve, but he drives on?

FLOSS. I lose.

TOM. And if you both swerve?

FLOSS. I still lose?

TOM. You share the loss of face. But if you drive straight on, what happens?

FLOSS. Well, he swerves, and so I win.

TOM. Or?

FLOSS. Boom.

TOM. So between, at worst, a loss of face, and – boom, what do you think you're likely to decide?

FLOSS. I'm thinking rationally?

TOM *gestures 'of course'.*

I swerve.

TOM. Mr Davis, do you agree with Miss Weatherby's analysis?

Pause.

PATTERSON. I do.

TOM. Presumably you're thinking the same thing.

PATTERSON. Yes.

TOM. And so knowing that the overwhelming likelihood is that Miss Weatherby will swerve, what do you do?

PATTERSON. I do the . . . Or, I guess . . . I might consider . . .

TOM. 'Might'?

Pause.

And by the same token,

Gesture to AL.

'Hey they won't really blow the mines, let's go in and arrest the leadership'. Or the rebels think: 'Come on, they'll never bomb the villages, but just one suitcase full of semtex and goodbye downtown'. Particularly if the next best option is some kind of mutual humiliation. As you might say also, take two superpowers, and a conflict over one side's missiles on a small cigar-shaped island off the other's coastal waters, and because the choice is standing firm or losing face, you have two superpowers each trying to persuade the other they might be insane enough to stick to their position even if it ends with blowing up the world.

AL. But surely the Cuba crisis wasn't really like that.

TOM. No?

AL. No. What really happened was a perfectly reasonable compromise in which the Soviet Union removed their missiles in exchange for the US not invading Cuba. Which was what they really wanted all along.

TOM. Right. So how might we have found out what was really wanted here?

Pause.

PATTERSON. Well, we didn't ask too many questions.

TOM. No. But I was interested in Miss Weatherby's rhetorical device. 'You say . . . ceasefire?'

FLOSS. Cessation.

TOM. ' . . . but I hear surrender'. Which in that form is a kind of accusation: you claim to be asking for suspension of hostilities, but you won't be satisfied until we've given up. But if, say, Miss Olsson was drawing up a diplomatic brief for the Swedish UN delegation, she might use the same device to explore the gap between both sides' positions and their interests.

GINA. I'm sorry, I don't understand.

TOM. The difference between what the rebels say and what they really want.

GINA. What they say *is* what they want, presumably.

TOM. What, like the Russians say: 'I'm going to keep my Cuban missiles come hell or high water.' But we hear – what you really want is to protect your friend.

GINA *shrugs.*

FLOSS. I think . . . well I assume . . . what the Professor means is . . . They say they have the right to sell the mines to anyone they like, but we're actually hearing that unless the US cavalry arrives damn quickly the economy goes down the tube.

TOM. And on the other side?

AL. Well, they're saying they won't give up a square rock of their ancestral mountain, but I'm hearing what they really want is to share some of the benefits.

GINA. They would maybe like not to be exploited.

AL. Sure. As they wouldn't be if the government gave leasing rights to the Americans, with strings attached on profit share and wages and conditions and the like.

TOM. Good.

To GINA*:*

But the most interesting point was actually yours.

GINA. Oh yes?

TOM. That the rebels' real interest wasn't being legalised but in being seen as legitimately speaking for the native people. Now who else has a problem with legitimacy?

PATTERSON. Well, the government, with the United Nations.

TOM. So might there be a mechanism for both government and rebels to make themselves legitimate before each other and the world?

GINA. Well, you know, Professor, I would imagine that the government might call some kind of popular election.

TOM. I'll be jiggered. So why not just announce the date right now?

PATTERSON. Because there isn't any guarantee that the rebels won't intimidate the population.

TOM. But surely there's no problem for the rebels. They've the prospect of a civilian administration. The promise of free and fair elections.

FLOSS. 'Prospect'. 'Promise'.

TOM. Yes. And of course the problem is, as soon as either side suggests a swerve, the other side digs in.

JAMES. As is the way when driving dubious analogies towards each other at considerable speed.

TOM. Or alternatively, you might find a different game to play.

Slight pause.

Two guys arrested for a robbery. They're kept apart. Miss Weatherby is their interrogating officer. What does she do?

FLOSS. Well, what tends to happen in the movies is that you tell them both the other one is going to rat on them.

TOM. And if Mr Bek rats and Mr Neil stays silent?

JAMES. Mr Neil is jiggered.

TOM. And Mr Bek gets off scotfree. But if they both rat on the other one then it's only fair they get time off for cooperating with the police. So their choice is either staying silent and risking going down forever, or ratting for a shorter sentence if not getting off scot free.

JAMES. I'm ratting.

AL. Ditto.

TOM. Fine.

FLOSS. But that's not the best option surely.

TOM. No.

FLOSS. Because, presumably, if they do the best thing for the other one then they do better for themselves.

JAMES. Aha.

TOM. How so?

FLOSS. Because the real benefit of ratting is if the other guy stays silent.

TOM. Yes.

FLOSS. But that isn't going to happen.

TOM. No?

FLOSS. Because like in the other game the other guy is thinking the same thing.

TOM. Exactly.

FLOSS. So the real choice is both rat for a shorter sentence or both stay silent and go free.

TOM. So the dilemma is: they have to be assured the other guy is either nice enough or smart enough to work that out.

AL. No way.

JAMES. On either count.

TOM. So it all comes down to finding someone else who you can trust.

PATTERSON. Clearly this man has not heard of the three great lies.

TOM. Go on.

PATTERSON. The check is in the mail, my wife doesn't understand me, I'm from the UN and I'm here to help you.

TOM. But with this necessary caveat in mind . . .

PATTERSON. Surely, the moment that the ceasefire and the date of the election are announced, we assemble an international UN force acceptable to both sides, charged with monitoring the elections and the ceasefire, and we send it in.

TOM. And both sides walk off free.

GINA. But surely all of this relies on the idea that everyone agrees on what is best.

Pause.

TOM. Go on.

GINA. That always the rational thing to want to do is stopping fighting. Even if you are the underdog, and the only way of achieving your objective is the use of force. Whereas it might be if the choice is peace or justice it is better that peace waits a while.

Slight pause.

TOM. Does anyone agree?

FLOSS. I'd put it slightly differently. I'd say . . . the assumption isn't just that when peace and justice clash, you go for peace. It's that what you dismiss as just positions, as the rhetoric and emotional indulgence that you've got to clear away to find out people's real interests, that this is actually their hopes and dreams. And that those hopes and dreams are just as fundamentally an interest as how their government is run. You see, I don't think people should be asked to sacrifice their language or their culture or their

vision of the future for what you see as their immediate
self-interest . . . When what you're asking them to do
effectively is give up who they are.

GINA. Well, of course, this is the other side of the same coin.

FLOSS. Oh, is it?

GINA. He says: surrender principles for peace. You turn
everything into an issue of the individual. You express your
'feelings', you articulate your 'dreams', and behold the
water's clean, there's universal healthcare, your kids can
read and you're not living in a shanty town.

FLOSS. No, I don't think that's what I'm saying . . .

GINA. Whereas I would say that the consequence of treating
these things as a game is to ignore the fact that in this world
some people have much power whereas some do not. And if
the powerful extend an empty hand then the last thing that
the powerless should do is shake it.

FLOSS. Oh, no, I'm all for shaking hands.

GINA. And no doubt listening to the ocean, finding inner space
and reaching out to touch the hand that bites you.

Slight pause. NIKOLAI SHUBKIN, *42, speaks from the
audience.*

NIKOLAI. Um, might maybe I make brief point now Professor
Rothman on this conversation.

TOM. Professor Shubkin. Please.

NIKOLAI. All I care to say now . . . you must please excuse
my English . . .

TOM *demurs.*

. . . is this point. That now since 40 year we seem but to
have one choice – triumph of US imperialism or total
victory of worldwide working class. And so we play so
often driving car fast at each other so to see who first will
blink. Or if not all this time we sit down in our cell and fail
to work out what the other guy across jail courtyard plan to
do. But now maybe for brief moment we come out of cell

into bright ray of light at least. I say we pray we do not miss our chance.

TOM. I should explain that Professor Shubkin is a former member of the Institute of World Economics and International Relations of the Soviet Academy of Sciences, saw distinguished service in Afghanistan and is visiting with us this semester from the University of Krum.

Pause. AL *looks surprised.*

And of course you're both right, there are limitations to these theories. But nonetheless, they deal with something desperately important. Because as Professor Shubkin says, what is happening inside the Soviet Union and the Eastern Bloc gives the peacemakers – gives us – the chance not just to end the cold war but to confront those smaller but persistent and intractable dilemmas which could not exist without it. But as Miss Weatherby points out, unlike the cold war, to resolve these conflicts we are asking people to give up their dreams. Or at least, to change their dreams to ones that they can share with people they've been taught to see as less than human. To sacrifice their pasts in the interests of a better future.

Slight pause.

Which is why we've spent this time together. And why we've invited people like Professor Shubkin here to join us.

Pause.

I am instructed to remind all those who are leaving Santa Cruz this evening that if they haven't yet checked out they should do so now. And that for all parties there will be a glass of wine to celebrate the conclusion of the seminar. Thank you and good afternoon.

The seminar breaks up.

TOM (*to the* GROUP). Well, thank you all.

Acknowledgment.

JAMES. Oh, please, don't mention it.

FLOSS. Thank *you*.

TOM *punches* PATTERSON *on the shoulder.*

TOM. Hey and Special Representative Pat *Davis.*

PATTERSON. Any time.

NIKOLAI *appears from the* AUDIENCE; TOM *goes over to him.* JAMES *stands, takes out his business card and hovers.* PATTERSON *smiles, gathers his papers and goes.* GINA *puts her papers in her file.* FLOSS *opens a big notebook and makes notes about the session.*

TOM. Kolya. Thank you for your intervention.

NIKOLAI. I enjoy most greatly Mr Davis's three big lie.

JAMES. Ah well, in fact, you know / there is another –

NIKOLAI. Though in our country we have little bitty different style. One, all shops sell oranges on Monday. Two, all quota are complete on Friday. Three, come up from your cellars you have nothing to fear.

TOM. Well perhaps that too will change.

JAMES. Well, as I say / that's not the only –

TOM. Now, Kolya, you must meet Al Bek. Who's a post-graduate in international trade law here, and whose favourite saying is: There's never been a war between two countries with McDonald's.

GINA *shakes her head and goes out, catching* TOM'*s eye for a moment as he turns and goes out too.*

JAMES. Um, professor . . .

But TOM *is gone.*

AL. Hi. In fact / my folks –

NIKOLAI. How do you do.

AL. Presumably that was a set-up.

NIKOLAI. Set up?

AL. Presumably your intervention was previously planned.

Pause.

NIKOLAI. Professor Rothman most delightful man. He very much want to reassure me how all happenings here at Santa Cruz is most strict among ourselves.

AL. It's rare to meet someone from Krum.

Pause.

NIKOLAI. Well, certainly in upstate California.

In Kavkhaz:

Ot Kafkáziya li ste? [Are you Kavkhazian by origin?]

AL. I'm Kavkhazian by origin. But I don't speak the language.

NIKOLAI. Maybe you speak other language.

AL. No. My mother occasionally speaks Kavkhaz at home. And pop has got a Drozdhan joke.

NIKOLAI. So you born mix race?

AL. No. I'm single race. I was born in the Union of Soviet Socialist Republics. My mom's a half-hearted kind of Christian and my father's a lapsed Muslim. Now we're all American.

NIKOLAI. And your father's Drozhdan joke?

AL. What did Jesus tell the Kavkhars? 'Don't move till I get back'.

Slight pause. NIKOLAI *hasn't responded.*

Based on the presumption all Kavkhazians are lazy.

NIKOLAI. Yes, I know. And once again I am set up I think.

AL *smiles.*

But you also I suppose.

AL. Oh, yes?

NIKOLAI. In the James Dean movie they do not drive straight toward each other but side by side toward big cliff. But Professor Rothman version little bit much better for his game.

AL. Aha.

NIKOLAI (*turns to* JAMES). So sorry. I think I interrupt you.

JAMES. No.

NIKOLAI. Well, there she go.

> NIKOLAI *goes.* AL *looks round, and then goes out.* FLOSS *closes her notebook.* JAMES *is putting his business card back in his wallet.*

FLOSS. Is that a business card?

JAMES. Yes. Please.

> *He hands her the card. That's not what she meant.*

FLOSS. Oh, right. Well, after all . . .

JAMES. . . . it's what these jamborees are for.

FLOSS (*looks at the card*). So were you sent here by your University?

JAMES. No, I'm doing it on my own recognisance.

FLOSS. Oh, why's that?

JAMES. I was informed it would look good on my CV.

FLOSS. Ah. Right.

JAMES. All terribly disreputable.

FLOSS. No . . . No, I find it rather sweet. Like when we were saying what we thought we'd be in five years' time and you were the only person to say 'diplomat'.

JAMES. You found that *sweet*?

> *She takes a leaflet from her file and scribbles on it, circling a telephone number.*

FLOSS. So much so that I'd most appreciate it if you would call and let me know if you succeed. Or if you don't. Or if you decide that what you really want to do is something else.

> GINA *reenters with her suitcase, which she lays down and opens, to pack her files away.*

JAMES. You're with Helping Hand.

FLOSS. And doesn't that just say it all?

JAMES. You said you were an actress.

FLOSS. Yes I did.

JAMES. Helping Hand is a international aid agency run by
    Quakers.

FLOSS. There are quaker actors. And there are people who
    were actors who end up being something else.

JAMES (*with a nod towards* GINA). Like the scourge of
    Marxist fundamentalists.

FLOSS. Scourge?

JAMES. Most effectively I thought.

FLOSS. Well, it's an ancient argument.

JAMES. What is?

FLOSS. Free the streets or free your head.

JAMES. And you go for the latter.

FLOSS. I go for seeing them as complementary.

   She realises JAMES *is looking at* GINA. *Standing:*

   A most attractive Marxist fundamentalist.

   Slight pause.

JAMES. So hence, I had assumed, attached.

FLOSS. To a husband and a child. But neither I think entirely
    to her satisfaction.

   FLOSS *goes to* GINA *and puts her hand out.*

   Well, so long.

   A moment. Then GINA *shakes* FLOSS's *hand.*

GINA. Goodbye.

FLOSS. In fact, there is a game that actors play. You get in
    pairs and you shake hands. Then you shut your eyes, walk

backwards till you hit an obstacle, and then you move around the room, your eyes still shut, your hand outstretched, trying to find the hand you shook before. And do you know? It almost always works.

GINA. What, if you really 'listen' to the hand?

FLOSS. Well, obviously, you must believe it's possible. Otherwise, nothing works at all.

As she leaves, to JAMES:

I'd go for it. After all, it's what these jamborees are for.

She goes out. JAMES *and* GINA, *left a little uncomfortably alone together.*

JAMES. So, have you had a drink?

GINA. No.

JAMES. Can I get you one?

GINA. No thank you.

JAMES. You're off tonight.

GINA. 'Off'?

JAMES. Going.

GINA. So it would appear.

JAMES. To Stockholm.

GINA. Denver. But it would actually be Helsinki.

JAMES. 'Olsson'.

GINA. The capital of a country under foreign rule for 700 years.

JAMES. Know how you feel.

GINA. Good. In fact, Finland is the Swedish word. The natives call it Suomi.

JAMES. I never knew that.

GINA. It amuses us, when the world asks that we solve their problems. We're from a cold north country with a language

no one understands, known universally by the name
imposed on us by one imperial power and living by favour
of another, and, guess what, we are here to help you.

JAMES. In fact, it isn't the UN.

GINA. What isn't the UN?

JAMES. The third great lie.

AL *enters and approaches.*

GINA. Well, I always heard it as 'the Federal Government'. So
what's your version?

JAMES. Well . . .

AL. Good evening.

GINA. Evening. Well?

JAMES (*embarrassed*). Oh, well . . . maybe . . .

AL. What's happening here?

GINA. James tells a joke.

AL. Well, you know, the Irish.

JAMES. Uh, perhaps . . .

AL. Hey, man . . .

JAMES. As a married woman . . .

AL. Can this be the case?

GINA. Yes it is. How do you know?

Pause.

JAMES. You said so, when we had to introduce ourselves in
three well chosen sentences.

GINA. No, I didn't. As I don't.

JAMES. Well then I . . . maybe . . . there she goes.

Flummoxed, he goes.

AL. What joke?

GINA. The third great lie. I guess the porno version.

AL. 'I'm not going to come in your mouth.'

GINA. Precisely.

A slightly edgy pause.

AL. He was trying to make out?

GINA. Yes, I presume so.

AL. It's a funny way to go about it. After a weekend's concentrated training in the tactics of resolving seemingly intractable dilemmas.

GINA. I do not regard the two activities as comparable.

AL. Oh no? I'd say they were / absolutely –

GINA. In this I am with Mr Neil. For the last three days we have been plagued with inappropriate analogies.

AL. Oh yes?

GINA. An authoritarian dictatorship and a people's liberation movement are not in fact two criminals who have done a robbery together. They are not two young men driving cars.

AL. Nor are they resolvable by reaching out and touching British hippy actresses.

GINA *looks at* AL.

GINA. Well at least I guess she doesn't want to give the world a happy meal.

AL. So were you ever touched by feelings of compassion for the miserable and the oppressed?

GINA. Compassion's how you start, not how you stay.

AL. That's more about your anger.

GINA. Oh for heaven's sake.

AL. Because you see, if I was you I'd think there was a real space, now, to create a new kind of society, amid the wreckage of the places my folks came from. But of course to make that work you'd need to open up your mind, to take a leap into the dark, to accept that doing better means you can't do best. So that might not be of interest to you.

GINA *going to pick up her bags.*

GINA. Yes, well, I ought to . . .

AL. Hey. In fact, he oversimplified the game.

GINA. What game?

AL. The prisoner game. Both staying silent isn't actually the best, because you have to share the loot. The best is if I rat and you stay shtum and you're inside forever.

GINA. Aha. So reaching out and touching is not quite best after all.

AL. No, but it's better than the other options. And, hey, money isn't everything. And you end up walking free.

GINA. Well, I'll be jiggered.

AL. Just remind me, where d'you plan to be in five hours' time?

GINA. In five hours' time, I will be on an aeroplane to Denver.

AL. Oh, of course. Otherwise there's a risk you'd end up listening to the ocean.

A WAITER, *of Afghan origin, has entered with a tray of drinks. He hovers.*

GINA. In fact, there is another puzzle, much more telling than the prisoner's dilemma. Not about what other people think is true or false but how you ascertain what is objectively the case. You go into a room, and there are two unmarked doors. One door leads to a future of unbounded, wondrous possibility and the other to a bleak and miserable past. And there's two men in the room, one who always lies and one who always tells the truth. And they know which door is which, and which of them is which, and you don't. But there is one question you can ask to find out what to do.

AL. Well, you ask, 'What day is it today?'

GINA. You've only got one question.

AL. Ah.

WAITER. I think you'll find you say as follows: 'If I was to ask you 'what door should I go through?', what would you say?'. To which question, the truthteller answers 'that one'. And the liar answers 'that one' too. As of course, he lies about the fact he'd lie.

GINA. That's right. Thank you.

WAITER. You're welcome.

He turns to go.

AL. Hey, you could settle something else here.

WAITER. Yes?

NIKOLAI *enters as:*

AL. I have a friend who has a choice. She can take the easy option, do the thing she's planned. Or she can take a risk, for once, she can junk the plan and take a leap into the dark. So if you were me, what would you advise?

NIKOLAI. Oh, I'd say, Mr Bek, you would advise her to take the lazy way. But then I am Kavkhazian.

He takes a drink from the WAITER, *who smiles quizzically and goes out.*

This young man I discover is a mathematic student from Kabul. He come here when he realise real choice is no more communism-capitalism but the modern world or rule by mujahedeen. I wonder sometimes if that may be in our country too.

AL. I . . . hear you.

NIKOLAI. Ah. An interesting phrase. In English mouth, he mean 'Yes, I agree, but of course I cannot say'. While in America it mean, there's no need to repeat, I am rejecting what you say already.

To AL:

I think she hear you in American.

He goes out. AL *turns to* GINA.

GINA. I wonder if it's true, about the touch thing.

AL. Sorry?

GINA. It's a thing of Miss Floss Weatherby's. It's a bit like, how you work out what the other person's thinking. Or – in this case – what the other person's feeling, I suppose.

AL. Uh . . . do you mean . . . ?

GINA. You heard.

Scene Two

Eight years later. A church bell chimes the hour. The first floor of what appears to be a derelict house. We are in Drozhdevnya/ Drozhdania, the southern province of the former Soviet Republic of Kavkhazia.

On the floor, a car battery, electric leads, a power drill. A young DROZHDAN MAN *lies asleep on a mattress.*

Upstage, a NAKED MAN *is tied to a battered office chair with castors. He has an airport duty-free bag over his head, and a gag tied over it round his mouth. A hole has been torn in the bag for him to breathe, but he cannot see.*

As the chime completes its cycle, the trapdoor suddenly bangs open. The 1st DROZHDAN *leaps up as two people come through; a* 2nd DROZHDAN MAN *in his mid 30s and* KELIMA BEJTA, *who is 29. They are all informally dressed in cheap Western-style clothes, but wrapped up well against the cold. They speak in what they see as their national language, Drozhdani.*

2nd DROZHDAN (*Drozhdani*). Size dediyim kimi, o kishi hech tapınmas burada. [I told you, he's quite safe. No one will find him here.]

KELIMA (*Drozhdani, to* 1st DROZHDAN). Tamam, haradadır? [OK. Where is he?]

1st DROZHDAN (*Drozhdani*). Arkhadadır. [In the back.]

KELIMA (*Drozhdani, to* 1st DROZHDAN). Bir shey dedi mi? [Has he said anything?]

1st DROZHDAN (*Drozhdani, to* 2nd DROZHDAN). Sana dedikhlarimden bashqa yokh. [Only what I told you].

2nd DROZHDAN (*Drozhdani, to* 1st DROZHDAN). Yoldash, bu yoldash tugay-komutanı Bejta! [Comrade, this is Comrade Brigade-leader Bejta!]

KELIMA (*Drozhdani, to* 2nd DROZHDAN). Drozhdanja danıshır mı? [Does he speak Drozhdani?]

1st DROZHDAN (*Drozhdani*). Zannetmam.[Not as far as I know.]

KELIMA (*Drozhdani*). Ingilisja danıshır mı? [Does he speak English?]

1st DROZHDAN *shrugs.*

Do you speak English?

1st DROZHDAN (*Drozdhani*). Bir az. [Just a bit.]

KELIMA. So how much is 'az'?

2nd DROZHDAN. I think enough.

1st DROZHDAN *shrugs, acquiescing.*

KELIMA. OK. You tell him first he is in our country but he cannot speak our language and we do not speak language of occupying power. He speaks no English, is tough shit.

1st DROZHDAN. OK.

KELIMA. Second will be: you tell him that we know he spy.

1st DROZHDAN. Sure thing.

KELIMA *realises* 1st DROZHDAN *isn't writing any of this down.* KELIMA *takes a deep breath and takes out a spiral bound notebook in which she jots down headings.*

2nd DROZHDANI (*Drozhdani*). Avvali, ziyaareti 'purposes of tourism' ichin dedi. [At first he say his visit is for 'purposes of tourism'.]

KELIMA. Oh, yuh?

1st DROZHDAN. 'Great tourist paradise Drozhdania'.

2nd DROZHDAN (*Drozhdani*). Laakin indi [But now] 'I wish to speak to member of military council'.

KELIMA. And you tell him even so we think him Khavkhar spy and we have good right to kill him by first rule of war.

She rips off the sheet of paper and gives it to the 1st DROZHDAN. *In Drozhdani:*

Gatir onu. [Go fetch him.]

1st DROZHDAN. And *you* cannot tell him this?

KELIMA. How many women please are there on military council?

The 1st DROZHDAN *goes upstage, to push the* NAKED MAN *forward on his castored chair.* KELIMA *sees the leads.*

2nd DROZHDAN (*Drozhdani*). Majlis-i Askarin durushu nadir bu kishi haqqında? [What is the military council position on this man?]

KELIMA (*Drozhdani*). Khoshbakht deyillar. Bunlar na? [They are not happy with it. What are these?]

The 2nd DROZHDAN *smiles knowingly.*

2nd DROZHDAN. 'First rule of war.'

The 1st DROZHDAN *wheels the* NAKED MAN *forward.*

1st DROZHDAN. I speak for Comrade of Military Council! There is three things we say to you! First that as you will not speak forbidden tongue we do not speak tongue you make compulsory for us.

KELIMA *nods, graciously: the* 1st DROZHDAN *has put it rather well.* 1st DROZHDAN *leans into the man:*

1st DROZHDAN. We know how you are spy of Kavkhaz Military Intelligence – and so by rule of war we think OK we kill you. In fact, more than just OK, it is traditional.

The MAN *is squirming.*

But first we wire you up to nice car battery and bake your balls.

KELIMA *can't say anything but is furious.* 1st DROZHDAN *picks up the two leads and puts them together to create a short circuit with its ominous 'tzzzt' sound. The* MAN *shakes and quivers in desperate fear.* KELIMA *goes to the* 1st DROZHDAN *and drags him away from the leads and the* MAN.

1st DROZHDAN (*Drozhdani*). Bu na? [What's this?]

KELIMA *whispers angrily to the* 1st DROZHDAN.

2nd DROZHDAN (*Drozhdani*). Na olıyar? [What's going on?]

KELIMA *pushes the* 1st DROZHDAN *back towards the* MAN. *As the* DROZHDAN *says what she has told him to say,* KELIMA *scribbles something else.*

1st DROZHDAN. But so in place we do not make you martyr. In place you bear us message to your leadership.

2nd DROZHDAN *looks surprised,* 1st DROZHDAN *shrugs and* KELIMA *hands him the piece of paper.*

1st DROZHDAN. No talk no ceasefire till all prisoner release.

2nd DROZHDAN (*Drozhdani, to* KELIMA). Bunun Majlis-i Askarın tarafindan kaabul olajaını aminsin mi? [Are you completely sure this will be accepted by the Military Council?]

1st DROZHDAN. This words please you take back from 'tourist Wonderland Drozhdania'. Please understand?

The MAN *nods.* 1st DROZHDAN *looks to* KELIMA, *who makes the throat slitting gesture.*

OK, game over.

KELIMA *points downwards and goes down with the* 2nd DROZHDAN.

Well, buddy, it seem we do not bake your ball together after all.

KELIMA *comes back up, quickly. She hands a note to the* 1st DROZHDAN.

(*In some surprise.*) So what is this? Chapter10, verse 92?

He doesn't know what to do with the piece of paper. KELIMA *takes it and puts it in the* MAN's *hands, folding them round the paper, in a surprisingly careful and gentle gesture.*

2nd DROZHDAN (*in Drozhdani, from below*). Yoldash Tugay-Komutanı! [Comrade Brigade Leader!]

KELIMA *goes quickly downstairs.*

1st DROZHDAN. OK. You take now message home from Holy Book. In the name of God, the compassionate, the merciful.

Scene Three

Two months later. Finland. The living room of a middle-class house. The house is on the side of a hill, so the entrance is above and people coming from outside come downstairs. There are two floor level exits: one to a playroom; the other to a dining room and, we imagine, a kitchen beyond. The interior design is almost satirically Scandinavian: clean, clear, simple, scrubbed and stripped. There is a computer and a printer set up at a table, and some battered luggage in the corner.

A 12-year-old boy, JAN, *enters on the upper level and comes downstairs. He carries a schoolbag and is listening to rock music on headphones. He sings along to a late 90s British song, loudly, in English, but without much regard to the sense of the words.*

GINA *enters from the dining room with a tray of bottles of wine and water, and nibbles in bowls.* GINA *speaks to her son in Finnish.*

GINA (*Finnish*). Jan, ne tulevat pian. [Ah Jan. They'll be here soon.]

JAN *sits down at the computer, still singing.* GINA *gets in his eyeline and waves.*

Jan, mä sanoin, että ne tulevat pian! [Jan, I said, they'll be here soon!]

JAN (*Finnish, taking the phones off*). Mitä? [What?]

GINA (*Finnish*). Minä sanoin, että vieraat tulevat pian. [I said, the guests will soon be here.]

JAN (*Finnish*). Ai jaa? [Oh, yes?]

GINA (*Finnish*). Ja me tarvitsemme tämän huoneen. [And I'm afraid I need this room.]

JAN *'hmphs'.* GINA *goes into the adjacent dining room.* JAN *stands.*

JAN (*Finnish, calls*). Keitä ne on? [Who are they?]

GINA (*Finnish, off, calls*). Johan minä selitin. He ovat ulkomaalaisia, ja sinun pitää olla vieraanvarainen ja puhua englantia. [I've explained! They come from abroad. You will have to make them welcome with your English!]

JAN (*in English, to himself*). So I make our dear guests welcome *with my English*?

GINA *comes back in with a tray of glasses, as* JAN *spots the suitcases.*

JAN (*Finnish*). Joko ne on täällä? [They are here already?]

GINA. Two are here already. The other two are with your father.

She lays out glasses and nibbles as:

JAN. Hello, old chap. Hi there, old bean. Well, howdidoodi, pardner.

The front door opens upstairs and GINA*'s husband* ERIK *enters on to the landing with suitcases.*

GINA. Well, why not. If things go sticky, you might prove a conversation piece.

JAN. What's a conversation piece?

ERIK. I think your mother means a conversation *point*.

GINA (*Finnish*). Onko kaikki kunnossa, Erik? [Erik. Is everything all right?]

ERIK (*Finnish, with a so-so gesture*). Niin ja näin. [It is all right-ish.]

ERIK *puts down the suitcases and goes back out.*

JAN. So where are both other people now?

GINA. I'm afraid they're in your playroom. In impassioned conversation, when I look last.

JAN. They are *where*?

GINA. I told you.

ERIK *is followed back in by* ROMAN LITVINYENKO *and* NIKOLAI SHUBKIN. ROMAN *is in his mid-30s, stylishly but casually dressed; his English is good.* NIKOLAI *is now 50, also casually dressed, though as before in a more obviously East European style.*

ERIK. We have some troubles at immigration.

GINA. I thought we booked the V.I.P. lounge.

ERIK. Yes, so did we. Unfortunately we did not have quite the right accreditation.

ERIK, NIKOLAI *and* ROMAN *are coming down the stairs into the room.*

JAN (*to his* MOTHER). In my *playroom*?

GINA. Only for three days.

NIKOLAI. And plus we are a little underdress for V.I.Ps I think. Mrs Olsson, so pleased I am to see you one more time.

ROMAN. Still too maybe.

GINA. Of course not. Professor Shubkin.

ERIK. It really wasn't anything to do / with how you're dressed –

NIKOLAI. Kolya, I hope.

GINA. Then Gina.

ROMAN. You see, we are not entirely sure / how we are supposed –

GINA. Please, everything is fine.

ERIK. So, Roman, this is –

ROMAN. Your wife. I am so very pleased to meet you. I have heard so much from Nikolai Mikhailovich. From, Professor Shubkin.

GINA *puts out her hand to* ROMAN.

GINA. Gina.

ROMAN *shakes* GINA*'s hand.* ERIK *goes towards the drinks.*

ERIK. And, so . . .

JAN. Ahem.

GINA. And Jan, our son.

NIKOLAI. Well, hi there, Jan.

JAN. Well howdidoodi there old chum.

ERIK. And now, I'd guess we could all use / a drink –

GINA. Jan, your supper's in the kitchen. With the video.

NIKOLAI. Aha.

ROMAN. We see you soon again I hope.

JAN. Well, it is my house.

NIKOLAI. So long.

ROMAN. And where are – the others?

JAN (*as he goes*). They're in my playroom. In impassioned conversation, when my mum look last. So long.

JAN *goes.*

ROMAN. And are they also members of organising committee of the European Games?

ERIK. No, one of them is here for medical reasons.

ROMAN (*to* GINA). I know nothing about sports. We are terrified that we are called upon to prove our status.

NIKOLAI. No doubt fear which grip too our friend.

ROMAN. Well depending naturally with which disease you have afflicted him.

HASIM MAJDANI, 52, has entered from the playroom. He carries a briefcase and is in a suit and tie. With him is KELIMA, dressed in severe, faintly paramilitary dark clothing. She has a briefcase also.

HASIM. Good evening.

ROMAN. Nothing too disabling I am glad to see.

HASIM. I beg your pardon?

ERIK. Dr Majdani, who is Director of the Free Hospital at Bazarat or as you know it Basda Brod. And here for consultations on his medical responsibilities.

NIKOLAI. 'Free hospital'.

HASIM. Which is accuse I know that he is front for terrorism. In fact, I am arrest and throw in jail for being his director. But so happily I am release since two week now.

No one has allowed themselves to get close enough for handshakes to become an issue.

ROMAN. And . . .

KELIMA. I am Kelima Bejta and I am member of the political committee of Drozhdan Khalq Jabhasi.

ERIK. Drozhdan People's Front.

ROMAN. Of course.

NIKOLAI. And so what cover do our kind host find / for you?

ROMAN stops him with a gesture, as HASIM interrupts.

HASIM. And now please we are told who you may be.

ROMAN. I am Roman Litvinyenko. I am editor of Rámka. Which as you know translate as 'Frame'. And Professor Shubkin is deputy head of the Institute of Kavkhazian Military History at University of Krum.

KELIMA. Professor or maybe General Shubkin.

NIKOLAI. Certainly not General.

GINA. But it's fair to say they are both here with the knowledge and blessing of the government in Krum. As are you with the knowledge and the blessing of the DPF.

HASIM. Well, knowledge, certainly.

ROMAN. We are here to resolve unrest in Drozhdevnya, province of former Soviet Republic of Kavkhazia.

KELIMA. We are here to discuss legitimate demand of Drozhdan people for self determination.

ERIK (*gesturing to drinks*). So, would you care to . . .

ROMAN. Thank you. I would very much like a glass of wine.

Partly in order to move, ROMAN *goes over to get his drink from* ERIK, *followed by* NIKOLAI.

NIKOLAI. Me also.

ERIK. Please help yourselves. Miss Bejta?

KELIMA. Do you have orange juice?

ERIK. Of course. Dr Majdani?

HASIM. I will have mineral water.

ERIK. Fine.

ROMAN *is helping himself at this moment, and so can pour orange juice for* KELIMA *and water for* HASIM.

HASIM. Thank you.

ERIK (*making to go*). And now, if you'll forgive me, I must attend to / making supper –

HASIM. Or if you forgive us, Mr Träsk, what we must do is to discuss all ground rule of our conversation here.

ERIK. In fact / this should be –

KELIMA. In particularly your own role in this as 'facilitator'.

GINA. In fact, this is not the role of Mr Träsk.

ROMAN. Oh, I had understood –

GINA. If anybody's it is mine.

Pause.

HASIM. Well, then, Mrs Träsk –

ERIK. And in fact my wife's name is Gina Olsson. Although it couldn't matter less.

GINA *raises the slightest of eyebrows, and goes and gets herself a drink.*

GINA. My husband is a senior official with the Finland Ministry of Sports, who was approached by a – concerned Drozhdani person at the Kavkhazian Olympic Trials. With the suggestion that the time might be ripe for resolution of the conflict between the two parts of Kavkhazia, and that the government might be thinking the same thing.

ERIK. While, happily, my wife met Professor Shubkin at the University of California some years ago. And is now deputy first secretary of the Southern European Section of our Foreign Ministry.

GINA. Although – of course – it couldn't matter less.

Pause.

NIKOLAI. So it agree we do not issue invitation to 'Drozhdan People Front'?

GINA. No, as I say, it came from a concerned Drozhdani. I think a businessman, I think somehow in the nickel trade. Which I pass on to Professor Shubkin, who pass it on to the Kavkhaz government. And via a naturally long and winding road of messages we end up here.

ERIK. So might we all sit down?

ROMAN. Agreed.

> *He and* NIKOLAI *sit.* HASIM *and* KELIMA *are consulting each other.*

HASIM. We agree also. But first it is most traditional among all Drozhdani people to present to hostess gift.

> *He takes a wrapped present from his briefcase and hands it to* GINA. GINA *sits and opens the present a little nervously. It's a lump of metal, crudely fashioned into a bowl shape.*

> It is ashtray, made from turret of water-cannon captured from occupying force by resisting freedom fighters following Massacre of Innocent at Bridge of Bazarat, of 22 November, 1990.

> *He sits, followed by* KELIMA.

GINA. Thank you.

ROMAN. There is of course no section of that sentence we do not contest.

NIKOLAI. Except maybe for 'it's an ashtray'.

> GINA *puts down the ashtray.*

HASIM. But maybe you don't smoke.

GINA. Well no. But, thank you.

> *Slight pause.*

> In fact, the events of November 1990 might be a good place to begin.

> ERIK *not sure about this.*

ROMAN. What do you mean?

GINA. I mean that sometimes it is good to start with something on which there are differences of opinion. Of course you have sharply different views of what happened on that day. But it is often useful nonetheless to describe your feelings when you heard about this, and indeed your feelings now.

Pause.

ROMAN. Miss Olsson, you are aware what happened at the bridge of Basda Brod?

GINA. Yes, of course I am.

Pause.

ERIK. First of all however we should start with everybody saying who they are, and what they expect and hope for from this meeting.

Pause.

ROMAN. Um . . .

GINA. And then it can be helpful too for each person to present their position to the others, say for five minutes, and then for someone else to summarize what they see as the fundamentals of the other person's case.

NIKOLAI. You mean, 'You say, I hear'.

GINA. Yes, if you like.

NIKOLAI. You change your tune.

GINA. Events in Berlin, Prague and Moscow change my tune.

KELIMA. No I'm sorry this is quite ridiculous.

Slight pause.

GINA. In what way?

KELIMA. We know what mean to 'tell each other what we want and hope and feel'. It mean all problems will be solve by people get to know each other better. Being nice and upfront, 'reach out I'll be there'.

GINA. No, actually / in fact –

KELIMA. So you clear away all 'rhetoric' and 'prejudice' and find we are so much in common – bouf we are all Scandinavians.

GINA. No of course that isn't what I'm saying.

KELIMA. No? But it is quite clearly what I hear.

Difficult pause. ERIK *glances at his watch then gestures to* GINA.

ERIK. Gina.

GINA. Please excuse us for a moment.

She and ERIK *go out.* NIKOLAI *takes out his cigarettes.*

HASIM. What means 'you change your tune'?

NIKOLAI. And she say. We meet since eight years in California.

Reenter GINA.

GINA. My husband apologises. He has had to go off to the kitchen. If our government is not to be accused of solving pressing international problems by a policy of deliberate starvation of its politicians.

A little helpful laughter. To KELIMA *then everyone:*

Look. I am sure that if we – if this thing is going to work it must be through an understanding of the way the world looks from the other side. As the events at – Bazarat or Basda Brod – make clear, there are two histories in contest, and I suspect we need to work out how those narratives collide. All we know is that there are two large populations sharing one small place who see themselves as having separate pasts but will have to share a common future. As surely whether it's a region or a country, no one thinks it could be right or possible to split it into two?

Pause. Neither side wants to agree first. Finally:

ROMAN. No of course not.

HASIM. See the map.

GINA. These are your meetings. You must run them as you wish. Maybe you have your own thoughts how we might begin.

She sits.

KELIMA. We have a document.

GINA. Good. Please.

HASIM takes out a document from his briefcase.

HASIM. It is naturally in our language.

NIKOLAI. I fear I am not speaking Gezhekh language.

KELIMA. This document is not in 'Gezhekh language'. It is in Drozdhani language.

NIKOLAI. No more I guess than Mrs Olsson.

ROMAN. Oh I can probably translate.

This is a bit of a surprise.

I was born and brought up in Fiore.

KELIMA (*quietly*). Sukhidat.

HASIM begins.

HASIM (*Drozhdani*). Drozhdan Khalq Jabhasının Siyaasi Komitesi tarafından bu prinsiplarin esaasi va danıshılmas oldunu sayır. [The Political Committee of the Drozdhan People's Front regards these principles as fundamental and non-negotiable.]

ROMAN. The Committee of the DPF view principles as basic and inviolable.

HASIM (*corrects*). Non-negotiable.

ROMAN. Non-negotiable.

HASIM (*Drozhdani*). Birinji, har ishghalchı quvvaların, Drozhdan torpaqtan geri chakmasiyla. [First, the withdrawal of all occupying forces from Drozdhani soil.]

ROMAN. First, withdrawal of our forces from – Drozhdani soil . . .

HASIM. In fact it is 'occupying force'.

NIKOLAI (*taking out a cigarette*). Beg pardon, is plan for you to read out all / this document?

HASIM *ploughs on. As* NIKOLAI *goes and gets the ashtray:*

HASIM (*Drozhdani*). Ikinji, Drozhdan Khalq Jabhasının,
Drozhdan Khalqın / tamsilchisi olmasını, Kavkhar
ishghalchılar tarafindan tanınması – [Second, recognition
by Kavkhar occupiers of the Drozhdan People's Front /
as the representative of the Drozdhani people –]

NIKOLAI. Forgive me. This appear it is our only ashtray. As
English it is our only common language.

He lights up. KELIMA *takes the document from* HASIM.

KELIMA (*translating the document as she goes*). Number two
demand. Immediate recognising of Kavkhar occupier DHJ
that is DPF in English as representative of Drozdhani people
in struggle for self-determination. Third is accepting of all
blame? maybe, responsibility, by occupiers for massacrè of
innocent at Bridge of Bazarat and for bringing of responsible
for crime to justice. Four please full reparation for historic
wrong performed to Drozhdan people who are forcibly
deport to Khazakhstan by Stalin for so-call collaboration
with invaders in Great Patriotic War. Five free all political
prisoner held by occupier in concentration camp. Or no I'm
sorry it 'releasing . . . '.

She doesn't know the English word, so shows the paper to
ROMAN.

ROMAN. Unconditionally. But as there is no concentration
camp in Kavkhazia, this demand I think we may accept.

KELIMA *snorts.*

And while on the topic of objective fact, there is no
'occupying force' repressing anyone in Drozhdevnya. What
exist there is a representative assembly, which the DPF
refuse to recognise, which control with other thing our
police. And when you say Drozhdan People's Front claim
mere right to self-determination I hear secession brought
about by terror, and joining up with another country namely
Gezhekhstan. And what you call 'Innocents' at Bazarat I
understand as rioter at town of Basda Brod who try to stop
a legal march in commemoration of our national heritage

and which turns into a pogrom of Drozhdnevnyan Christians if Ministry of Interior does not intervene.

KELIMA. Mr Litvinyenko, I have sister die in what 'you say riot I hear pogrom'. She is fifteen and she is sitting down on bridge and she is truncheon by your police and she fall to raging river underneath and she is drown. Like 37 other person. Sorry other rioters. So sorry actually children.

ROMAN. Miss Bejta, we have all suffered in this conflict. To suffer is not a privilege of just one side. In that, no one side has monopoly.

KELIMA. Oh, what? *You* suffer?

ROMAN. Oh, yes.

GINA. Now, this is getting nowhere / we should stop this now –

KELIMA. What, you *yourself*?

JAN enters from the dining room.

JAN. Excuse me, gentlemen and ladies. My pa requests the mindless terrorists and their hatchet-faced oppressors to come in to dinner.

There is a moment of uncertainty. JAN *looks to his* MOTHER, *then back to the* OTHERS.

Oh and he ask me to inform you of house rule. No business talking over dinner. Light general conversation only. That is, if you'd be so kind.

Slight pause.

GINA. You said – you said two things. One was: The police are responsible to the representative assembly which you'd like the Drozdhan people to recognise. The second is, Dr Majdani said that he wished the DPF to be recognised as representing the Drozhdani-speaking population.

Slight pause.

I wonder, after dinner, if it would be interesting to make a simple list of what you see as the actual interests of those you represent. And see how many words turn up on both.

Slight pause. HASIM *stands.*

HASIM. Well, it must be a simple list. If it is in my English.

NIKOLAI *stands.*

NIKOLAI. I find it hard to think what I may tell my wife. As first thought I think I say I have dirty weekend with my secretary. But I know that she will say: Don't give me all that shit, you can't fool me. You're off in Scandinavia negotiating peace agreement with DPF.

NIKOLAI, HASIM *and* ROMAN *follow* JAN *into dinner.* GINA *stops* KELIMA.

GINA. I'm sorry. I got off on the wrong foot.

KELIMA. 'Wrong foot'?

GINA. Of course you're right, about 'reach out I'll be there'.

KELIMA *looks at* GINA.

KELIMA. You know this so-call 'representative assembly' in boycott by majority?

GINA. I do.

KELIMA. As all Drozhdan 'representative' are force to pass Kavkhazi language test and swearing oath of loyalty to Kavkhaz state?

GINA. Yes, so I understand.

KELIMA *makes to go.*

KELIMA. OK.

GINA. It must be difficult for you.

KELIMA (*obviously*). How so?

GINA. I gather there was a battle on the military council. Some of the men felt there was no possibility of finding common ground, between you and the ethnic Kavkhars. I understand it was a close-fought thing. But you won through.

KELIMA. You know if this thing fail, then we say we are never here.

She goes in to dinner. A moment, then GINA *follows.*

Scene Four

Two days later. There is considerable evidence of last night's discussions – empty bottles, dirty glasses and crockery, full ashtrays. There is a map of Kavkhazia on the floor – in the southern region of Drozhdevnya, the Kavkhar population areas have been marked in one colour, the predominantly Drozhdan areas marked in another, and the mixed areas – covering most of the region – cross-hatched in both. NIKOLAI is still in pyjamas and a dressing gown, sitting at the computer typing in a document from a manuscript. JAN too is in his night things, watching over his shoulder.

JAN. What are you doing?

NIKOLAI. I type up document.

Pause.

JAN. What's it about?

NIKOLAI. It is called Draft Declaration of Shared Principles.

Pause.

JAN. So why is it in English? Why not in your language?

NIKOLAI. We have two languages. And nobody from their side learn our language and no one from our side learn theirs.

JAN. You know, if my writing was as bad as that, I'd be sent off home to do it all again.

NIKOLAI *laughs. He leans back, lights a cigarette.*

NIKOLAI. In fact, this is not my writing. It is the Drozhdan man.

JAN. So why can't he type it out himself?

NIKOLAI. Well, you know when Jesus down on earth what he tell to Drozhdhan.

JAN. No, what?

NIKOLAI. 'Don't move till I get back.'

A moment, then JAN *gets it and laughs.*

NIKOLAI. So what d'you know about Kavkhazia?

JAN. Well, it's a country of eight million people, nestling in the shadow of – Berushka mountains, main industries heavy manufacturing and agriculture, main resources low-grade nickel and brown coal.

NIKOLAI. So, do you know of Russian doll, with smaller inside bigger?

JAN. Surely do.

NIKOLAI. Well, biggest doll is former Soviet Union. Inside for many years is Republic of Kavkhazia. Now Kavkhazia is proper country too, but inside him is largely Muslim province called Drozhdevnya which is where big mines are but which think, hey, now we may be proper country also. Unfortunately, in Drozhdevnya is Kavkhazian minority of maybe third who do not think is quite such fabulous idea. And so by open up big doll all little doll blow open too.

JAN. And you all come here to sort this out?

NIKOLAI. We all come here to sort this out.

He taps the document. GINA *is coming down the stairs with shopping bags.*

JAN. And so, the future of your country is depending *on my mother*?

NIKOLAI. Sure.

JAN. Well, bloody hell.

GINA. 'Dependent' on your mother. Well, it's good to know one's son has trust.

She sees JAN*'s still in night things.*

Even if he's not yet dressed at eleven in the morning.

JAN *looks over to* NIKOLAI, *who stands, also in his nightwear, looking a little sheepish.*

Well, Professor Shubkin is at important work.

She begins to collect glasses.

NIKOLAI. I'm sorry, um . . .

GINA. No, please. You must feel free –

NIKOLAI (*gesturing at the glasses*). I meant . . .

GINA. Well, ditto. Is Roman up?

NIKOLAI. I think he is maybe back in kitchen making breakfast.

To JAN:

We are very late last night. Except for Miss Bejta. Who is sensible and goes to bed.

GINA. Dr Majdani?

NIKOLAI. Well, I think he still . . .

Sleeping gesture.

JAN. Well, you know what Jesus told the Drozhdans.

GINA. Sorry?

JAN. 'Don't move till I get back'.

GINA *looks fiercely at* JAN.

It's his joke.

A moment.

GINA. Good.

GINA *takes her shopping out. There is a moment of solidarity between the two under-dressed men.*

JAN. I thought it was quite funny.

NIKOLAI. Hey. You know I say the Drozhdans – well, some Drozhdans – want to be part of next door Muslim country.

JAN. Gekhestan.

NIKOLAI. Gezekhstan. Who major product is root vegetable.

JAN. I see.

NIKOLAI. And the joke is: Why do Arabs get all oil and the Gezhekhs get all turnips? And the answer is – the Gezhekhs got first pick.

JAN laughs, then stops.

JAN. Don't get it.

NIKOLAI. Well the point / maybe is that they are bit –

GINA enters, a little flustered, from the dining room.

JAN. Mum, what?

GINA. He's praying.

NIKOLAI. Who?

GINA. Dr Majdani. I was just, um, tidying . . . and then I saw him kneeling head down on the floor.

NIKOLAI. You know, he says he is not so religious . . .

HASIM enters from the dining room, looking round.

HASIM. Good morning.

OTHERS. Morning.

HASIM. Forgive me, I have lost a . . . ah.

He picks up a pen, which NIKOLAI has been using, from by the computer.

NIKOLAI. Oh, I'm sorry – uh, I must have . . .

HASIM. No matter. It is only sentimental value. It is given me by President Gaddhafi.

He goes out into the playroom.

GINA. Aha.

JAN makes to go. NIKOLAI doesn't know how to print the document.

NIKOLAI. Um . . .

JAN *picks up* NIKOLAI'*s tone and turns back.*

JAN. You want it printing out?

NIKOLAI. Yes, please. Five copy.

With aplomb, JAN *sets the printer to print and bashes the button. As soon as the first sheet begins to curl out of the printer:*

JAN. Well, *I'm* going to get dressed. It is eleven in the morning.

He goes upstairs.

GINA. You know, he's got a rather – delicate, dry sense of humour.

NIKOLAI. Your son?

GINA. Well, yes. But I was thinking of –

NIKOLAI. Colonel Gaddhafi.

GINA. Hm.

NIKOLAI. A medical professor. As you say, good sense of humour. Quite easy sometime maybe to forget.

GINA. To forget?

NIKOLAI. On 22 November, in riot, after bridge is clear, our police see children running downstairs to cellar. They chase after, and find cellar floor covering in film which look like greasy water. With big door at other end, where last boy stand there, waiting, till police all safe inside, then toss match on to petrol. Boy no older maybe than your son. So when you say alternative to peace is tearing us apart, I say, maybe this happens now already.

GINA. Would the Drozhdanis see it like that?

NIKOLAI. Let me tell you how I see it. In mid-ages yes we are occupy by Ottoman. In modern era we are occupy by Russia then by Soviet Union. Under Stalin many churches in Agari region smash up and even under Brezhnev period Soviet army use cave monastery for target practice. So now at least we get to own our country for first time. For us, Drozhdevnya our Jerusalem. Do we hand it back to Turk?

Slight pause.

GINA. I hear you.

NIKOLAI. Sure. But do you hear in British or American?

KELIMA and ERIK have entered above. They come down the stairs.

KELIMA. Good morning.

GINA. Morning.

ERIK. We've been walking.

KELIMA. How do you say, healthy powers?

GINA. Therapeutic.

KELIMA. Therapeutic powers of countryside.

GINA. I'm glad. I'll tell the others you're back.

To ERIK:

Dr Majdani's in the playroom.

She goes out. ERIK *goes into the playroom.* KELIMA *and* NIKOLAI *nod at each other.* KELIMA *goes to the computer and looks at the hand-corrected version of the document.*

KELIMA. This is new version of shared principles?

NIKOLAI. Yes.

KELIMA (*picks up a sheet*). Revisions since yesterday.

NIKOLAI. Cosmetic changes merely.

Enter GINA *and* ROMAN *from the dining room,* HASIM *and* ERIK *from the playroom.*

ROMAN. Good morning.

KELIMA (*Drozhdani*). Ah Hasım, bu na? [Ah, Hasim. What is this?]

ROMAN. Is there a problem?

KELIMA *looks to* ROMAN, *then to* HASIM:

KELIMA (*Drozhdani*). Bir problem var. [There is a problem.]

HASIM (*Drozhdani*). Na var? [What's the matter?]

The following three speeches together with the subsequent two speeches.

KELIMA (*Drozhdani*). San onları matnı dayıshtırttın, khalq khalqlara, sechkilar qurallları, dil mesalası. [You have let them change the text – people to peoples, election rules, language question.]

HASIM (*Drozhdani*). Bunlar yüzeysal . . . [These are cosmetic . . .]

KELIMA (*Drozhdani*). Yoldash Hasım, bu dayıshtırmalar yüzeysal deyillar! [Comrade Hasim, these are not cosmetic changes!]

Simultaneous with:

ROMAN (*to* NIKOLAI, *in Kavkhaz*). Kakvó stáva took? [What's going on?]

NIKOLAI (*Kavkhaz*). Nyamám ponyátie. [I've no idea].

ERIK*'s looking at the printout.*

ERIK (*a little offhand*). Um, English, please. Is this – is the italic what you've not agreed?

ROMAN (*looking*). No, the italic is what we have agreed.

ERIK. Some way to go.

ERIK, ROMAN *and* NIKOLAI *turn to* HASIM *and* KELIMA.

HASIM. Yes, I am sorry. With maybe . . .

ROMAN. Yes?

HASIM. One or two so small amendments also.

Pause.

ROMAN. Hasim, we stay up to four a.m. on this.

NIKOLAI. We are here three days. We are book to leave tomorrow.

KELIMA. I have no doubt that booking may be change.

Hiatus. ERIK *decides to try and break it.*

ERIK. Call me when you'd like lunch.

ERIC *is going, as the phone rings. Although* GINA *instinctively moves to answer it,* ROMAN *gets there first.*

ROMAN (*Kavkhaz*). Álo? Izvinyávaite, gréshka. [Hallo? Ah. Sorry.]

Hands the phone to GINA.

GINA (*takes the phone*). Hallo.

In French:

Je vais bien. Mais, comment vas tu? Oui, en effet, ce n'est pas le bon moment. [Just fine. But how are *you*? Yes, in fact, this is a bad moment.]

Pause. ERIK *goes out.*

Je suis désolée, je n'en sais rien. Ce soir peut-être. À bientôt. [I'm afraid I don't quite know. Tonight maybe. 'Bye.]

She puts down the phone.

KELIMA. Do you expect a call?

GINA. No, I . . .

KELIMA. I'm sorry, I mean Mr Litvinyenko.

Slight pause. NIKOLAI *is looking quizzically at* GINA, *wondering about her call.*

ROMAN. Yes. I am waiting for a call from Krum.

HASIM. I think that we agree / we make no calls –

ROMAN. On what subjects are these 'small amendments'?

HASIM. We must insist on 'peoples' not 'people' of Drozhdania.

ROMAN. I see.

KELIMA. Nor can we accept election under international observation. It must be international scrutiny.

NIKOLAI. This is small amendment?

KELIMA. And it is not right of children to be taught their Drozdhan language. But *by* Drozhdani language.

GINA. As the medium of instruction.

KELIMA. As is not I think 'cosmetic change'.

ROMAN. No indeed not. So we must discuss it.

NIKOLAI. This is everything we amend last night.

ROMAN. But there is one thing we do not amend. We agree we finish by tomorrow morning. I do not make plans to change my flight.

KELIMA. We'll work in playroom. It's easier to spread out papers.

ROMAN *looks to* GINA.

GINA. Yes of course.

HASIM, KELIMA, ROMAN *and* NIKOLAI *go out with their documents.* GINA *goes to the phone. She is picking it up when* JAN *comes downstairs, dressed. She puts it down.*

JAN (*Finnish*). Hei, äita. [Hi, mum.]

GINA (*Finnish*). Hei, kulta. [Hallo, darling.]

JAN (*Finnish*). Missä ne ovat? [Where are they?]

Enter ERIK.

GINA (*Finnish*). Pelihuoneessa. [In the playroom.]

ERIK (*Finnish*). He ovat vielä pelihuoneessa? [They're in the playroom?]

Enter ROMAN, *as:*

GINA. Mitä Kelima kertoi sinulle, kun kävitte kävelyllä? Kertoiko hän esimerkiksi, miksi he esittävät 'hard cop soft cop' mutta väärin päin? [So what did Kelima tell you on the walk? Did she talk about why they're playing 'hard cop soft cop' the wrong way round?]

ROMAN (*wryly*). English, please.

GINA. Sorry.

ROMAN. Do you have an English dictionary?

GINA. What, English-English?

ROMAN. Preferably.

JAN. Yes, I've got one. Granma Olsson gave it me for Christmas.

GINA. Could you get it please.

JAN *goes out.*

ROMAN. Do carry on.

ERIK *and* GINA *glance at each other.*

Unless you were having light general conversation under dinner table rule. But I think not.

GINA. Oh why not?

ROMAN. You look far too animated.

ERIK. No, we were talking about Kelima Bejta.

Slight pause.

ROMAN. And maybe how very strange that she is on faction of military council who support these talk, but here she plays 'hard cop'. Whereas Majdani, who is sent here clearly as her minder, appears to give up most.

GINA. Yes that did surprise us.

ROMAN. Did she say anything about it on your walk?

ERIK. I . . . don't think I could say.

JAN *has reentered.*

JAN. Here's the dictionary.

ROMAN. Thank you.

JAN. Are you near a breakthrough?

GINA. No.

JAN. I am very eager not to miss it.

ROMAN. So are we.

JAN. What are you looking for?

ROMAN. We need a word a little short of 'friendship'.

JAN starts to speculate. ERIK, *firmly:*

ERIK. Thank you Jan.

JAN grins and goes out.

GINA. Um . . . 'amity'?

ROMAN. In fact, the situation is deceptive.

ERIK. Oh?

ROMAN. You're right of course. You make list, and you find that often you are thinking the same thing. Both sides want guarantees against discrimination by the other. We are loyal to majority Kavkhazian, they to majority Drozdhanian. We are both loyal to the principle of equal democratic rights for all.

GINA. That's very elegant.

ROMAN. Big tip. I think she thinks you think that you can weaken her. On grounds of woman solidarity. For you she seem like western feminist, because she is angry with how men behave. But in fact she thinks concerns of western feminists are essentially trivial. A luxury, set against real problems of the world.

He goes out. ERIK *looks at the telephone, looks at* GINA.

GINA. So now he tells me.

Scene Five

The next day. In fact, early the following morning. Luggage in the corner. ROMAN, HASIM, KELIMA *and* NIKOLAI. ROMAN *is reading out a draft.*

ROMAN. OK. Recognising both their historical affinities and distinct traditions and allegiances, the parties declare their loyalty to the principle of a multi-ethnic, democratic future for the peoples of the Bela River basin. Accordingly, the Kavkhaz Government recognises the Drozhdan People's Front / as the legitimate –

NIKOLAI. Which we change to 'acknowledge'.

HASIM (*Drozhdani*). Öyle mi? [Did they?]

KELIMA (*Drozhdani*). Öyle, yadda sakhların mı? [Yes, you remember?] It is in exchange for word 'legitimate'.

Enter GINA *with a tray of food and drink.*

ROMAN. . . . so, 'acknowledges' the DPF as the legitimate representative of a substantial section of the population of the province. It agrees to the setting up of a Commission of Amity to investigate and to report on past acts of violence, intimidation and harassment, by all parties, particularly the events of / late November –

NIKOLAI. Particularly but not exclusively . . .

ROMAN. . . . the events of late November 1990 on the bridge connecting Bazarat with Basda Brod. While for its part the DPF dot-dot-dot-dots the use of violence in pursuit of its political ambitions.

Slight pause.

NIKOLAI. And so here we are once more.

HASIM. It cannot be 'renounce'.

NIKOLAI (*wearily*). Why not?

KELIMA. Because 'renounce violence' make all invalid our armed struggle.

NIKOLAI. Why?

HASIM. 'Renounce' mean it was wrong. You renounce drug-taking or adultery.

NIKOLAI. But without you will accept the Kavkhaz sovereignty, there is no guarantee without renouncing you do not take up arms again.

HASIM. It cannot be.

ROMAN. It must be. I am told it must be so by Krum.

Pause.

KELIMA. This is your call.

ROMAN. Correct.

KELIMA. We agree we do not make consultation.

ROMAN. We agree that we seek agreement that will fly. I tell you that this will not fly. You tell me it's your bottom line and I think it's good we know your bottom line won't fly.

KELIMA. And this from horse's mouth of / your beloved President –

ROMAN. I speak to chief of staff of President Petrovian. In fact, I speak twice. I call him back. It must be 'renounce violence'.

Enter ERIK, *with more food. He looks at* GINA *questioningly. She mouths 'renounce'.*

KELIMA. This does not happen.

ROMAN. And it cannot be declaring 'resistance' to terror, how can you resist something you are doing?

HASIM. But if we are 'terrorists' / then how can –

ROMAN. It must be 'renounce'. Implying –

HASIM. We know what it implies.

Pause.

GINA. Could it not . . . have you explored 'both sides'. Or 'all sides'. Or 'all citizens'.

ROMAN. Gina, one side is the state. How can it be 'both sides'.

KELIMA. This is impossible. I'm so sorry.

Pause.

GINA. All I'm saying is, there might be room / for some adjustment –

ROMAN. No there is no room. We accept 'ceasefire' not 'cessation'.

NIKOLAI. 'Complementary' not 'precondition'.

ROMAN. It is – it has no practical effect. It is a form of words.

KELIMA. Oh sure yes. We tell those women whose sons and husbands die for free Drozhdania we renounce them but OK because just form of words.

HASIM. I say again. So sorry. It may not be unilateral renounce.

Pause.

ROMAN. Then I'm so sorry also. We have run into the sand.

Pause.

KELIMA. This is revenge for our small amendments.

ROMAN. No. Oh no.

KELIMA. This is because we add one 's' to one word.

ROMAN. No it is not.

KELIMA. This is because we want our children to be brought up speaking their own language.

ROMAN. No. But I must say – ?

KELIMA. Yes? Yes? What must you say?

GINA (*sensing what this is provoking*). Um, Roman . . .

ROMAN. No, I must say this. This happen for two days. We take one step, they take one step, then they demand we take one more step just as they jump two step back.

KELIMA. We are here for principle negotiation. Not class for dancing.

ROMAN (*furious*). No, it is not dancing class. It is the method of the rug market. It is the tactic of the souk.

This is the worst thing to say.

It is you who are aggressors. It is you who must renounce your violence if you must gain what we are offering today. How might it any way be otherwise?

HASIM *stands, goes and picks up* KELIMA's *luggage.*

HASIM. I think we must leave to catch our plane after three hour. There is no point now to go to bed.

KELIMA. They are never serious.

HASIM. We wait upstair.

KELIMA. I fetch my overnight thing.

KELIMA *goes into the playroom as* HASIM *heads for the stairs.* JAN *appears in a dressing gown and pyjamas.*

ROMAN (*to* GINA). You see.

HASIM. This is very obvious planned provocation.

GINA. Please, Hasim. Please.

ROMAN. You see, to find something common . . .

NIKOLAI. This is absurd.

ROMAN. It is necessary first to be . . .

HASIM (*bumping into* JAN). Ah. Hallo.

GINA. Jan. What?

JAN. I need a glass of water.

ROMAN. I'm so sorry. Do we wake you?

JAN. No. What's happening? Are people going home? Have I missed the breakthrough?

KELIMA *enters with her overnight bag.*

GINA. No, you haven't missed the breakthrough.

ROMAN. You see, to find something common it is needed first to be something there to find.

KELIMA. Which since noted date in 1990 it so hard to do today.

NIKOLAI. Well we can say today will not be noted date for anything.

Pause.

KELIMA. I'm hungry. I wait here.

She comes down and takes a chocolate, offering the plate to JAN.

JAN (*taking chocolate*). Thanks.

KELIMA. Maybe time now for dinner speaking rule and 'light general conversation'.

HASIM *comes down and sits. Silence.*

ERIK. I've a question, I've been waiting days to ask. Does anyone – did anybody realise that the 22 November was the anniversary of John F. Kennedy's assassination?

They look at him, taken aback.

I ask because, here in the west, anyone who was alive then is supposed to remember where they were when they heard the news. I am 13 and as it happens I am dressed up in a ballgown and a long blonde wig as I am a Princess in a boys' school play.

Slight pause.

JAN. You mean like Mr Gorbachev.

NIKOLAI. Like Gorbachev?

ERIK. We became a little conscious even more about the dates of things when Jan is born in March 1985. It is the day that Mr Gorbachev is elected leader of USSR.

GINA. My 13th birthday on the other hand is the day of landing on the moon. I remember, nobody that day is very interested in my party.

Slight pause.

'One giant leap for mankind'.

Pause.

Jan, go and get your water.

JAN goes out. Silence. GINA, suddenly tempted, reaches for a cigarette. She changes her mind. She takes a chocolate instead. Finally it's NIKOLAI who can't bear it.

NIKOLAI. As it happen, I am in Dallas on that day.

GINA. For the assassination?

NIKOLAI. No, at time of . . . Bridge, riot or whatever. It is commemorative conference on historiography of cold war. What will happen maybe if Lee Harvey Oswald miss.

ERIK. Sounds interesting.

NIKOLAI. Not so much – to me – as news come in from Basda Brod. But there is one good joke. The Moderator say that if Krushchev shot in place of Kennedy, we can agree at least that Mrs Krushchev will not marry Aristotle Onassis.

A little laughter. Silence. Then:

HASIM. Actually . . . I am also in America at this time. In New York for colloquium of legal implications of treatment of HIV.

This sounds potentially threatening.

GINA. Ah . . .

HASIM. And there is good joke told there also.

Unnoticed, JAN enters with his water.

HASIM cont.) Why does New York get all lawyers and San Francisco all homosexual? And answer is: San Francisco gets first pick.

ROMAN, NIKOLAI, ERIK *and* GINA *laugh, interrupted by:*

JAN. Oh, *right*. I see.

HASIM. What?

JAN. It's the same as why the Arabs get the oil and Gezhekhs get the turnips.

NIKOLAI. Uh . . .

JAN. Because . . .

He picks up that this may not be a good idea as:

KELIMA. . . . like San Franciscans, Gezhekhs will choose first.

JAN. Yes.

KELIMA. It is often told about Drozhdans and brown coal.

NIKOLAI (*attempted rescue*). Hey. How you define moral dilemma for Kavkhazian. Your customer pay you thousand lek note in place of a 500. The dilemma – do you tell your partner?

HASIM (*not good enough*). Ah yes, of course. 'Tactic of souk'.

An edgy moment. ROMAN *decides to deflect:*

ROMAN. But the Russians have the best joke. A man from the south applies for a good job. The Russian says, this is all fine, you seem most excellently qualified, but there is just one thing. Where do you come from? And the man says, oh, I am Drozhdanian. And the Russian says, oh dear, I'm sorry, this is an obstacle we cannot surmount, as everybody knows the Drozhdanians are very very lazy. And the man says, no, no, it's OK. You've got it wrong. It's the Kavkhazians that are very lazy. The Drozhdanians are crooks.

HASIM. Ah yes of course. This is like Drozhdan father who has son who comes one day and says, father I want to marry Kavkhaz girl, and her father says, this is terrible, you want your kids to be too dumb to steal?

Angry, KELIMA *stands and goes to get another sandwich.*

But maybe joke offend our company.

NIKOLAI. Particularly not exclusively our hostess.

GINA. Oh I am not offended.

NIKOLAI. Good.

The wind has gone out of the moment. KELIMA *sits. Another silence.*

GINA. But it shows the problem does it not? If you cannot make your minds up whether your neighbours are more dishonest than than they're lazy than they're dumb.

Pause. EVERYONE *is taken aback by* GINA*'s aggression.*

ERIK. But of course, a joke can often represent / a deeper truth –

GINA. And as everyone points out you have been here three days, and everyone agrees we must find common ground because the alternative to finding it is yet more sons and husbands dying pointlessly, and yet more wives and daughters too. But of course how can you find a compromise which inevitably must rely on trust with people who faced with choosing between war and peace choose bloodshed as first pick?

Slight pause.

But maybe I make too big a point of something that is actually very trivial. After all, what do they say about the Finns?

NIKOLAI. What do they say?

HASIM. No sense of humour.

GINA. I am so sorry. We did our best. We are down to the difference between two words. I can't see what else we can do. Come, Jan, let's go to bed.

KELIMA *intervenes.*

KELIMA. I have a joke. In 1944 when Drozhdan people are expel by Stalin to Khazakhstan. And whole villages of lazy Drozhdanis dumped in middle of marshy land where no cattle graze and no wheat may grow. And Russians say,

that's that. But since five year they come back and behold
Drozhdans have plant rice and fed themselves. So Russians
take all rice and transport Drozhdans to great height
mountain where they put them down to die. But still
Drozhdans maybe too stupid still to comprehend and they
build igloo and kill mountain bear to eat. And five year is
pass and Russians come back once again, and Drozhdans
still alive so smash their igloo and move all Drozhdan to
baking desert. And again behold, stupid idle Drozhdans
raise goat and feed off meat and milk and when three year
is pass and Russians come back and say, Look. If these
dumb idle Drozhdans still survive, now maybe we send
them all back home. And so / at last they go back –

ROMAN *comes quickly in.*

ROMAN. Of course. They get back home to find their farms
are occupied since 1944 by wicked Kavkhars and their
house is smashed up and their livestock dead. And yes what
happen to the Drozhdan people is most terrible. But they are
not the only people who will suffer then or now.

KELIMA. Well so you say.

ROMAN. Well so I say.

KELIMA. But it is not quite what I hear.

Slight pause.

ROMAN. Oh no?

KELIMA. I hear . . . you are from Sukhidat. Maybe your
parent or your grandparent are ones who occupy a
Drozhdhan flat or farm.

ROMAN. Maybe.

KELIMA. And maybe they don't smash it up at all, but leave it
clean, with bread and salt upon the table for those who
return. And who knows perhaps despite this Drozhdan
children who are tired and starving from their journey
maybe still they call your grandmother bad names and spit
at her.

Pause.

And I hear you say: 'OK, my grandmother she does not suffer quite so much as yours. But she suffer still. And now she is – 80? 85? – she sit alone and think what happens now if children and grandchildren of those Drozhdans win their independence. What will happen to her now?' Is this not what I hear?

ROMAN. Of course.

Pause.

And you say this. 'Fifty years ago, it is hard between us but it is not so bad as now. Even though then as now all Kavkhars idle dumb dishonest and all Drozhdans stupid lazy crooks. But now you say: we cannot speak our language to our children. Now you exclude us from all civil life and hospitals and schools. After everything you do to us, is it any wonder that you cannot trust us not to kill your grandmother? So please dear Mr Litvinyenko, how may we convince you you are wrong?'

Pause.

GINA. You know the choice. It's possible that either side will win. It's possible – it's likely – neither side will actually lose. But surely there's a better option for both sides.

ROMAN (*to* KELIMA). And so of course I hear you when you say that you cannot 'renounce' the only tactic open to you.

Slight pause.

But maybe now you may reject it.

KELIMA. 'Reject' imply it is not happening I think.

ROMAN. That's true.

ERIK. So then if not 'reject', 'forsake'?

HASIM *looks to* KELIMA.

GINA. Or if not 'forsake', 'relinquish'?

Slight pause.

Voluntary. Not conceding rights or principles. Not implying it was wrong before.

HASIM *looks up to* KELIMA.

KELIMA. We can accept 'relinquish'. Yes. Agreed. What next?

JAN *looks questioningly at his mother.* ERIK *smiles.*
NIKOLAI *looks at the document.* GINA *nods to her son.*

Scene Six

*Three months later. Geneva. The hall in Geneva airport
prepared for a ceremony. Two small tables with flags, a lectern
with the crest of the US Secretary of State. Logos of the OSCE,
the EU, the UN and the Governments of Finland and
Switzerland on hangings behind. Two* ORDERLIES *are setting
out chairs.* PATTERSON, *now in his late 30s, is checking what
they're doing against a chart in his hand. He is also talking on
a mobile telephone.*

PATTERSON. OK. Do you have an atlas? Open it at Europe.
Can you find Italy? Place your finger on the bottom and go
upwards, there's a kind of oval bit that may be brown or
squiggly to indicate it's mountainous, and a little blue
smudge, with the word 'Geneva'. Beside which is a little
airplane in a circle. That's where we are.

He reangles a pair of chairs. The ORDERLIES *notice this.*

Now take your finger rightwards to Vienna – it's possible it
may be spelt W – I – E – N. *You bet* on purpose. And thence
to Budapest – you have that? – then to Bucharest, yuh, you'd
think they'd make them sound more different, and then the
Black Sea which is strictly neither *then* . . . you got it.

He notices the flags on the table. Picks one up. To an
ORDERLY:

Hey. There's a no flag rule.

The ORDERLY *looks blank.* PATTERSON *tries German:*

PATTERSON (*German*). Keine Fahnen! [No flags!].

1st ORDERLY (*French*). Je parle Français. Nous sommes à Genève. [I speak French. This is Geneva.]

PATTERSON (*French*). Nous avons convenu. Pas de drapeaux. [There's an agreement, no flags.]

1st ORDERLY (*French*). D'accord. [Fine.]

The 1st ORDERLY *takes the flags out.*

PATTERSON. But I understand the stationery is subtly colour-coded.

Checking on his chart:

Oh. And the wrong way round.

Down the phone:

No, it's your dime.

Slight pause. PATTERSON *changing the pens, blotters and agreement binders round, as he speaks:*

Why? Well. The deal was done in Finland, so the alternative to Geneva is the Outokumpu Declaration and it was felt to be in the interests of amity for it to be proclaimed somewhere the signatories could pronounce.

To the 2nd ORDERLY, *in French, as the* 1st ORDERLY *returns:*

Hey, are there not supposed to be some flowers? (*French.*) N'y a-t-il pas de fleurs? [Aren't there flowers?]

2nd ORDERLY (*Italian*). Prego? [Excuse me?]

PATTERSON (*French, to the other* ORDERLY). N'y a-t-il pas de fleurs? [Aren't there flowers?].

Ist ORDERLY. I hear you. They will come.

Enter KELIMA. *She is dressed formally. She has a plastic information pack issued for the day.*

PATTERSON (*down the phone*) Oh, no. Our role in this is essentially ceremonial. Didn't you hear? We are in the Hour of Europe.

Sure. Again.

Handing a chair to the 1st ORDERLY:

I think you'll find the Gezekh Consul has a wheelchair.

1st ORDERLY. Fine.

The ORDERLIES *go out.*

PATTERSON. No, that's not you. No, in this case, you can take it that I *am* the Secretary of State.

He snaps his phone shut. To KELIMA:

Major US media. Talk about spoonfed.

KELIMA. I am Kelima Bejta.

PATTERSON*'s phone goes.*

PATTERSON. Excuse me.

PATTERSON *answers his phone.*

KELIMA. Drozhdan People's Front.

PATTERSON (*down phone*). No, not President. He's General Secretary. So it's 'Mr General Secretary'.

Phone off. To KELIMA:

Sorry. Pat Davis. You're here for the handshake.

KELIMA. Yes.

PATTERSON *puts out his hand.*

PATTERSON. Well, hi.

KELIMA. Uh, in fact, you are . . . ?

PATTERSON*'s phone goes.*

PATTERSON. Oh heck.

He answers the phone:

No, it's all agreed. No uniforms and no regalia. And certainly no arms, however small.

Snaps phone shut. Noting KELIMA*'s outfit:*

Which appears to be all fine and dandy here. I'm sorry, you were saying?

KELIMA. I understand there would be . . . other people.

Enter GINA, *also smartly dressed for the ceremony, with her pack.*

PATTERSON. Sure, and so there are. Hey. Gina *Olsson.*

GINA. Well, Patterson. You've come some way.

PATTERSON*'s phone rings.*

PATTERSON. You too. One second.

Down phone:

What?

KELIMA. Secretary of State?

GINA. Um . . .

PATTERSON. I'm *on hold*?

GINA. Why don't you switch that off.

PATTERSON. Hey. Great idea.

He switches off his phone.

GINA. Is this the handshake?

PATTERSON (*approaching her*). Yes this is the handshake.

GINA. I thought, the secretary of state . . .

KELIMA. This is not secretary of state?

PATTERSON. As if.

KELIMA. 'I *am* the secretary of state'.

PATTERSON. Ah. I mean, I am speaking for the secretary of state. As opposed to a state department spokesman, or a 'senior state department source'. Or indeed 'a source close to the Secretary of State'. Which actually is the Secretary of State. Who proceeds here from the Sheraton in precisely one hour seven minutes time. To preside benignly over the historic handshake between the Secretary General of the

Drozhdan People's Front and President Y. V. Petrovian of the Republic of Kavkhazia.

GINA. One hour?

PATTERSON. Pretty nearly.

GINA (*realises*). Central Europe summer time.

KELIMA. Excuse please. You two know each other?

GINA. Yes. We met at the same seminar where I meet Kolya Shubkin.

PATTERSON. At which point Miss Olsson is somewhere to the left of Kim Il Sung.

To KELIMA*:*

How's the hotel?

KELIMA. I am not yet in hotel. I am only just arrive.

GINA *looks questioningly.*

PATTERSON. There was a problem with Miss Bejta's visa. So. Is there not a Mr Olsson?

GINA. His name is Träsk. He is not here.

PATTERSON (*taking out his phone and dialling*). Oh? I'd better let him know.

He looks at his phone.

KELIMA. You switch it off.

GINA. Who know?

PATTERSON. Hey, right.

He switches it on. Checking against his chart, he goes to a distant part of the room and removes a chair.

The Secretary of State. I think he'd worked out some light diplomatic joke about 'who wears the striped pants here'.

He's dialling.

GINA. Well, we must be grateful for small mercies.

PATTERSON. Hey, he does his best.

GINA. So this where I am sitting?

PATTERSON. Sure. Oh, by the way, he is left-handed. And whatever he calls you, you call him 'Mr Secretary'.

He's through.

Hi. Yuh, I switched it off. Ain't that the truth.

Pause.

OK. Yuh, sure. I'll be right there.

Snaps phone shut.

KELIMA. There is problem?

PATTERSON. Well, yes. In the sense of 'no'. In the sense of – well, we're running late. But apart from that, everything is . . . fine and dandy.

Nervy pause.

Hey do you know the original idea of handshakes is to demonstrate there's nothing in your hand.

He goes out. The WOMEN *look at each other, deciding not to speculate as to what* PATTERSON *has heard on the phone.*

KELIMA. So. Erik does not come?

GINA. No. He says it is 'my moment'.

KELIMA. But everything I so much hope is 'fine and dandy'.

Very slight pause.

GINA. Oh, completely. Um . . . Drozhdani colours, I presume?

KELIMA. That's right.

GINA. You look most elegant.

KELIMA. You sound surprise.

GINA. No, I'm sorry. Why shouldn't you look elegant.

KELIMA. Just because I am major terrorist by regular daytime employment.

GINA. But we hope not for too much longer.

KELIMA. If so because of you.

GINA. Oh, no.

KELIMA. Hey. You may settle now a question. Majdani and I think you get so angry with all jokes, so everyone think, hey, at least we have one thing in common, unlike dour Miss Finland, at least we all have sense of humour. Is this not correct?

Pause.

GINA. Yes, you're correct.

KELIMA. Then maybe I am right about another little thing.

GINA. Oh, what?

KELIMA. That when I ask if everything is fine and dandy in your life, and you say 'Oh completely', it is in the sense of 'maybe not quite absolutely', no?

GINA *takes out a packet of cigarettes.*

GINA. Well, I'm sure we're not supposed to smoke.

KELIMA. You smoke?

GINA. Very rarely. Not at home. Do you want one?

KELIMA. No. I give it up. Your good example.

Slight pause.

So. Again. My question?

GINA *lights up.*

GINA. You know how tiresome it can be when people claim political activity is just a way of masking problems in your private life. As no doubt they say you are a revolutionary because your borders were invaded as a child.

KELIMA. My borders *are* invaded.

GINA. I meant, your personal . . . The theory that, if you're abused . . .

KELIMA. Of course. Or you want a husband really.

GINA. Or to kill your father.

KELIMA. Or to have a child.

Slight pause.

GINA. And do you?

Pause.

KELIMA. My hope above all things is that today will come to pass.

ROMAN *has entered, dark and formal in his suit.*

GINA. Roman.

ROMAN. Here you are.

GINA. What's happening?

ROMAN. So no one's told you.

KELIMA. What?

GINA. Don't say – your people have pulled out of the agreement.

ROMAN. Yes.

KELIMA. What?

ROMAN. As a consequence of a violation of the terms of the ceasefire.

KELIMA. Violation?

ROMAN. By the siezing of off-duty police clerk as a hostage. As retaliation for a raid on a Fiore club which claim to be Islamic centre but police say front for drugs.

KELIMA. Oh, and naturally/ everybody is arrested –

ROMAN. And by the time police clerk is release Drozhdani Kavkhars occupy assembly in Fiore demanding that agreement is abort.

KELIMA. To which provocation doubtless Petrovian gives in.

ROMAN. No, actually he orders the army to retake the building. It is his generals who refuse. Not least because a Kavkhar group called the Society for St Demetrius organises for 500 people to be lying on the steps.

GINA. But the police guy was released?

ROMAN. Oh yes.

KELIMA. And he is harmed?

ROMAN. No, he is not. But by / this time . . .

GINA. And the agreement?

ROMAN. I overhear the black guy say – 'game over'.

GINA. But they can't do that.

ROMAN. They've done it.

GINA. And the Secretary of State?

ROMAN. Apparently he is held hostage by world press in Sheraton. They are busy try to find a way to slip him out.

GINA. O God.

ROMAN. I'm sorry.

GINA. So am I.

> *They both look at* KELIMA. KELIMA *goes and picks up the duty-free bag she brought in. She holds it out to* GINA.

KELIMA. I buy this for you. Celebration of big mountain which we climb. Don't worry, it is not ashtray.

> *She turns to* ROMAN*:.*

> Lie one: Beneath, we all the same. Lie two: Both sides just fine and dandy as each other. Lie three, of course, that this is spontaneous action by Society of St Demetrius.

> *She goes out.* GINA *is left there with the bag.*

GINA. The check is in the mail. My husband doesn't understand me.

ROMAN. And the common ground is big enough for everyone.

GINA. What do you mean?

ROMAN. Room enough for us, of course. Those who enjoy fine food, fine wine, fine conversation. But problem is the people that are leave behind. The Islamic Centre and the Society for St Demetrius. So-called 'extremists' on both sides.

Slight pause.

GINA. So is it true? That Petrovian set up this demonstration?

ROMAN. Look, the guy was just a police clerk. I don't think he even wore a uniform.

GINA. Nothing happened to him.

ROMAN. But he doesn't know that, until it has not happened. Tied, blindfold, terrified, doubtless threatened and abused in a language that he doesn't understand. In fact, of course, it is much worse before. When you don't know what they'll do to you.

Slight pause.

GINA. 'In fact'.

ROMAN. That's right. In fact.

Pause.

They think because of this I make no compromise. That I am hardcop of all hardcop, because I am keep blindfold naked as a prisoner in tourist paradise Drozhdania. But I realise that like us Drozhdan are divided and unsure of what to do. Which makes me even more determined to succeed.

GINA. What was your experience?

ROMAN. Oh not too terrible. They decided I am a better messenger than martyr. And the message was – let's build the bridge we burn today.

He stands, goes to the doorway, turns back.

You have a fear. That you discover real problem with your search for common ground. That when people see it they don't want it. As so nice Miss Bejta say. Not that we do not know each other. But that we know each other all too well.

He goes out. GINA sits and looks at the empty chairs and tables around her. She opens the airport bag, looks inside. She closes the bag, looks upwards, closes her eyes. Then she takes out her mobile phone and dials.

GINA. Kelima, it's . . .

She realises it's an answermessage.

OK. It's Gina. Just to say . . . All I can ask you, is to believe this thing was worth it. And if there is the faintest prospect of it happening, I promise I'll do anything to make it come to pass.

She clicks the phone shut, opens the bag, takes out a tube of Toblerone, unwraps it and bites off a piece. NIKOLAI enters to GINA, late, in his suit, with his suitcase and a huge bouquet of flowers. He sees GINA, her mouth full of Swiss chocolate.

NIKOLAI. Miss Gina Olsson. So where is everybody else?

GINA (*wiping her mouth*). They ratted.

End of Act One.

ACT TWO

'A second requirement of a potential settlement
is that it is Pareto optimal. This condition is fulfilled
for settlement A if no alternative settlement B exists
such that at least one party is better off with B than with A,
while at the same time no party is worse off with B
than with A.'

Jon Hovi
Games, Threats and Treaties, 1998

'The Americans thought a few meetings would solve it,
as if it were a personal quarrel. In reality, we were divided
by a mountain of corpses.'

Aliya Izetbegovic
President of Bosnia, 1995

'The Chechen–Ingush Republic is a sovereign state,
created as a result of the self-determination of
the Chechen and Ingush peoples . . . The Chechen–Ingush
Republic has the attributes of a sovereign state:
citizenship, a crest, a flag, a national anthem and a capital.'

Declaration of Chechen Congress,
November 1992

'I am the President. I am His Excellency, the President
of Palestine. What you want to do is make me
the head man of a village council.'

Yasser Arafat,
December 1993

'In the First World War, over 80 per cent of battlefield deaths
were combatants; by the 1990s over 90 per cent
of war-related deaths are civilians, killed in their own homes
and communities . . . The least dangerous place
to be in most contemporary wars is the military'.

Miall, Ramsbotham and Woodhouse
Contemporary Conflict Resolution, 1999

ACT TWO

Scene One

Two years later. Drozhdan\Drozhdevnya. Summer. A checkpoint on the edge of government-held territory. A large pile of medical supplies stands upstage, marked with the Aid Express logo. It has been broken into, with boxes opened and packs and even pill boxes opened to check on their contents, left on the ground. LEN, *a Black British UN soldier in his 30s, is keeping his eye on the boxes, watched warily by a* KAVKHAZIAN SOLDIER. *A* 2nd KAVKHAZIAN SOLDIER *comes in to speak with him. Downstage,* FLOSS *waits. She is 49, dressed in a T-shirt and long shorts. Enter* NIKOLAI SHUBKIN, *in field military uniform. He has papers.*

NIKOLAI. Well why Miss Weatherby.

    FLOSS *turns.*

FLOSS. Ah good afternoon. Are you the commanding / officer –

NIKOLAI. But this is disappointing very much.

FLOSS. I beg your pardon?

NIKOLAI. You clearly do not readily remember me.

FLOSS. Uh . . . no?

NIKOLAI. My name is Shubkin. Last time we meet in University Santa Cruz.

FLOSS. Oh . . . yes. At the peace seminar.

NIKOLAI. How all things turn about.

FLOSS. Ain't that the truth.

NIKOLAI. In fact, not for first time. Since two years I am with Miss Gina Olsson of Finland in hush hush backstage negotiations.

FLOSS. Yes, I know. They failed.

NIKOLAI. Yes, sadly.

FLOSS. I understand that she was very disappointed.

NIKOLAI. I am very disappointed also.

FLOSS. Professor Shubkin / we need to talk about –

NIKOLAI. But now here it is, we meet inside this crazy situations. And charming Mr Neil from Dublin Town also. What place for class reunion.

FLOSS. 'Mr Neil'?

NIKOLAI. So they are telling me.

FLOSS. Who's telling you?

> NIKOLAI *waves his papers. They are faxes. During this the* 2nd KAVKHAZIAN SOLDIER *goes out.*

NIKOLAI. Our people naturally fax copy of your passport. You may think this very primitive. Once we are scanning all such thing and sending digitally from mobile phone. Sadly since five month terrorist have track equipment from Iran which mean you are on satellite for more than minute plus a half and boom. This of course in quite watertight major international arms embargo. Now I am right that Aid Express is once call Helping Hand?

FLOSS. That's right.

NIKOLAI. New name more hip and up-to-date.

FLOSS. Well, yes. Professor Shubkin / are you in charge –

NIKOLAI. Colonel, but please, Kolya.

FLOSS. Are you in charge of these men here?

NIKOLAI. I am in charge of many men. Now maybe you please tell me now of what is situation.

FLOSS. As you are aware, Aid Express is an accredited aid body supported by the UN, transporting desperately needed medical supplies to Estafan.

NIKOLAI. Of course. Maybe I question little bit so desperate need.

FLOSS. And this mission has full authorisation from the Kavkhaz high command.

NIKOLAI. Of course I know this. I am part of Kavkhaz high command.

FLOSS. And that this consignment has sat here for eight hours in the heat being so-called 'checked' by so-called 'tax officials' – all of whom went off at least an hour ago to 'telephone for fresh instructions', all because these men – your men – refuse to let supplies through to the people who, yes, desperately need them.

NIKOLAI. And why is this?

FLOSS. You know full well. Because you want the Drozhdans to release a group of ethnic Kavkhazians whose presence in Estafan is effectively the population's only guarantee of safety from your guns. A solution neither to our liking nor frankly in our gift.

NIKOLAI. Even though this happen often now in both direction. Even though since three days we let 200 Muslim wife and children free from Novye Ghla.

FLOSS. Yes I am aware of what occured in Novye Ghla.

NIKOLAI. But you do not prefer be ethnic cleansing aid assistant.

FLOSS. No, frankly not.

NIKOLAI. You wish instead all people here to live in peace and harmony and love is all you need.

FLOSS. Colonel Shubkin, this is not a time / for jokes –

NIKOLAI. No, I agree. But in this time I fear Miss Weatherby you are quite way behind.

Slight pause. He looks at his watch.

Since – hour plus thirty minute, terrorist leadership agree to our quite reasonable request to evacuation of innocent civilians. Convoy approach. All sorted. No one is telling you?

FLOSS. What? It's all sorted?

NIKOLAI. Sure.

FLOSS. And the convoy's on its way?

NIKOLAI. Of course. Now I remember. Floss.

Slight pause.

FLOSS. Yes.

NIKOLAI. Short for 'Florence'.

FLOSS. Yes.

NIKOLAI (*looks at fax*). But in full, Miss Florence Hazel Weatherby.

To FLOSS:

Trust me.

Enter JAMES *followed by a 33-year-old aid worker,* TREVELYAN, *the group's 24-year-old translator,* EMELA, *and the* 2nd KAVKHAZIAN SOLDIER.

JAMES. Floss, this is intolerable.

FLOSS. Trev. What's happening?

TREVELYAN. They've heard back from 'headquarters'. Apparently, they have to take it all apart.

NIKOLAI. So maybe now glitch come.

FLOSS. What, all of it?

JAMES. And if there's one pack or tablet over . . .

NIKOLAI. Well why Mr Neil. Long time no see.

JAMES. Uh – yes?

NIKOLAI. From Dublin Town.

JAMES looks to FLOSS.

FLOSS. It's Professor Shubkin.

NIKOLAI (*puts out his hand*). Well it since many years back naturally.

JAMES. Professor?

FLOSS. Colonel. But – but still.

JAMES. Ah. Right. Right. Well.

Discommoded, he shakes NIKOLAI*'s hand.*

TREVELYAN. Colonel, your men are demanding that they take the delivery apart, so they can 'inspect it', and it would be very helpful if you could tell them / that this is interference with an authorised humanitarian consignment . . .

NIKOLAI (*to* 2nd KAVKHAZIAN, *in Kavkhaz*). Kakvó stáva took? [What's going on?]

2nd KAVKHAZIAN (*Kavkhaz*). Tryábva da naprávim revíziya na kartónite s taká naréchenata 'houmanitárna pómosht'. [We need to inspect the so-called 'medical supplies'.]

NIKOLAI (*Kavkhaz*). Sufsém priémlivo e. A te otkázvat? [Sounds reasonable enough. And they refuse?]

2nd KAVKHAZIAN (*Kavkhaz*). Tézi hóra sa mnógo ópaki. [These people are not reasonable.]

JAMES (*to* EMELA). Well?

EMELA. He ask what is big issue here. He say: We wish to search the so-called medical supplies. He say: Sounds reasonable to me. So what's the problem? He reply: These people are not reasonable.

NIKOLAI (*Kavkhaz*). Razbírate li kafkázki? [You understand Kavkhaz?]

EMELA. A little.

NIKOLAI (*Kavkhaz*). Áma víe anglichánka ste? [But you are English?]

EMELA. I live now in England.

NIKOLAI. And your name?

EMELA. Emela.

NIKOLAI. Ah. So many Drozhdan western passport. Sometimes it seem compulsory.

EMELA. My mother is Drozhdani. My father is originally from Baku. I am language student now since three years at Bristol England. Now I work you see for Aid Express.

NIKOLAI. I make just general point. I understand that DPF high command consist of weightlifter who defect to USA at Seoul Olympics, Afghan mercenary who work in New York driving minicab since five years and barman voted number one at cocktail shaking three years running by some most important London magazine. While so-call Drozhdan so-call Ambassador to European Union live in Paris on proceeds of narcotics prostitution and arm smuggling and has not set foot here since he is small baby.

JAMES. I am not I have to say that interested in all of this.

NIKOLAI. Oh, no? It is for these people you deliver medical supplies.

TREVELYAN. No not those people.

NIKOLAI. Ah. You think they all end up with sick and wounded lying now in hospital.

JAMES. Well, not if your men have their way.

NIKOLAI. Once more I think that like Miss Weatherby you way behind. Happily our demand are met. Our citizens are now release. Just when they will be here, you may deliver your supply.

JAMES *looks at* FLOSS *who nods.*

JAMES. What, unconditionally?

FLOSS. Seems so.

NIKOLAI. Only naturally subject to inspection.

TREVELYAN. Oh, right.

JAMES. Oh I see. You mean as soon as you've ripped off what you want then you will graciously allow us to deliver the remainder to the sick and dying.

FLOSS. James.

NIKOLAI *is angry.*

JAMES. Well, what d'you think / that this is all about –

TREVELYAN. Jim, let it go.

FLOSS. Hear hear.

NIKOLAI (*to 2nd* KAVKHAZIAN SOLDIER, *in Kavkhaz*). Ímate li spíssuka na sudurzhánieto na kartónite? [Do you have the manifest?]

2nd KAVKHAZIAN (*Kavkhaz*). Éto. [Here it is.]

As NIKOLAI *looks at the manifest.*

JAMES. Here we go again. Just like at Kudjali.

FLOSS. Well, this is Kavkhazia.

EMELA. He reads the manifest.

NIKOLAI (*Kavkhaz*). Kakvó e [What is] 'anti-histamine'?

2nd KAVKHAZIAN (*Kavkhaz*). Ne znam. [I don't know.]

Simultanous with:

JAMES. I don't see why we should make involuntary donations.

FLOSS. Don't you?

JAMES. Why, do you?

FLOSS. Yes, when we're nearly there.

NIKOLAI (*Kavkhaz*). Da, imenáta zvouchát káto meditsínski. [Well, it all sounds plausibly medical.]

EMELA. He seems convinced.

NIKOLAI. Washing powder? Washing powder is a medical supply?

TREVELYAN. Yes of course it is. If you're in a lice and rat-infested hospital without power or water \ then obviously –

NIKOLAI. But I am quite content this medicine will be deliver now.

FLOSS. You are?

NIKOLAI. What say Woody Allen? 'You've got to have a little trust in people'.

JAMES. Faith in people.

FLOSS. Quite.

NIKOLAI*'s mobile phone rings. He answers. In Kavkhaz:*

NIKOLAI. Álo, Shóubkin na telefóna. [Hallo, this is Shubkin.] (*English.*) Ah. Hallo. How good to hear you. Yes of course. So I expect. Where are the buses? Yes so we do same thing at Novye Ghla. Of course I understand.

End call.

Another old friend comes her way.

(*To* 2nd KAVKHAZIAN SOLDIER, *Kavkhaz*) Ídvat. Vurvéte da gi posréshtnete. [They're coming. Go and meet them.]

2nd KAVKHAZIAN (*Kavkhaz*). Slóusham goospoodíneh. [Yes, sir.]

He goes out. TREVELYAN *goes to speak to* LEN, *the UN soldier.*

FLOSS. Thank you.

NIKOLAI *looks to* JAMES.

JAMES. Yes, thanks. As Woody Allen says . . .

NIKOLAI. So Florence-Floss. And what you playing at since all these years go by?

FLOSS. Oh, you know. This. Trying to be helpful without getting killed.

NIKOLAI. But James when we last meet you will be government advisor?

JAMES. Sure. I was persuaded to change course.

NIKOLAI. By maybe Florence Weatherby?

JAMES. Yes, as it happens.

NIKOLAI. And you maybe married now?

FLOSS. What, to each other?

NIKOLAI. Well . . .

JAMES. No, we're neither of us married.

FLOSS. And, I can't remember . . .

NIKOLAI. My wife she die since one year and one half. Something go bad from small operation in her ear.

FLOSS. I'm sorry.

NIKOLAI. So since I fail to solve my country problems, now I must try to keep him in one piece.

JAMES. That's how you see it?

NIKOLAI. Like US civil war. 'One nation under God'.

FLOSS. But surely, that's the problem.

NIKOLAI. Surely. Two nationality, two religion, two language and two alphabet. Sadly, one range of mountain, one big river, one coastline and one coal field, one electric grid. Even now we do big deal with Volkswagen for nickel alloy and smart guy from Texaco find perfect route for Baku crude to run through Kavkhaz pipeline to Black Sea. But yet without we agree we split our country up from top to bottom NATO send you people home and bomb us back to stone age.

JAMES. Well, that's not quite how / I'd put it –

NIKOLAI. But maybe Mr Neil think we so primitive barbarian we in stone age time already.

JAMES. No of course I don't.

NIKOLAI. It is believe all Drozhdan women work for foreign NGOs are prostitute. Also that all UN troop from Africa have HIV. I fight against these most unprogressive view.

FLOSS. Len isn't African. He comes from Lewisham.

NIKOLAI. Ah Star Wars Two.

FLOSS. Beg pardon?

NIKOLAI. The Empire Strike You Back.

Enter the 2nd KAVKHAZIAN SOLDIER.

2nd KAVKHAZIAN (*Kavkhaz*). Slézoha ot dzhípa i ídvat.
[They are coming from their fourwheel.]

Both KAVKHAZIAN SOLDIERS *aiming guns at the
entering group:* KELIMA, *in paramilitary uniform, and a
small family: a* FATHER, MOTHER, *wheeling a* YOUNG
MAN *in a wheelchair and a 10-year-old* BOY.

KELIMA. Nikolai Mikhailovich.

NIKOLAI. Kelima Bejta. You bring us sample group in
fourwheel.

KELIMA. Yes.

She goes to shake his hand. The 2nd KAVKHAZIAN
SOLDIER *stops her.*

What's this?

2nd KAVKHAZIAN (*Kavkhaz*). Tryábva da ya pretúrsim. [We
should search her.]

NIKOLAI. He wants to search you.

KELIMA. The idea of handshake is to show that you have
nothing in your hand. But fine. Maybe you search your
people also. Maybe you start with guy in wheelchair.

NIKOLAI (*taking the point*). OK.

2nd KAVKHAZIAN (*Kavkhaz*). Pokazhéte ni poné váshata
líchna kárta. [At least we must see your papers.]

NIKOLAI. He say . . .

KELIMA. Yes, I know. Sure. They your people. Naturally they
have ID.

NIKOLAI (*Kavkhaz, to the* SOLDIER). Da, preglédaite
dokouméntite im. [Yes, check their papers.]

The 2nd KAVKHAZIAN SOLDIER *goes to look at the
family's papers.* TREVELYAN *is returning to the main
group.*

JAMES (*to* FLOSS). So where are all the others?

NIKOLAI. They keep in bus as hostage. As we do just the same.

KELIMA *hands him binoculars. He looks offstage.*

FLOSS. Hostage for what?

JAMES. The consignment, we must hope.

KELIMA. And also till we cut our deal.

NIKOLAI. What deal?

TREVELYAN. What's this?

FLOSS. Don't know.

NIKOLAI. We have deal already. You release our people there is medical delivery.

KELIMA. We need more things besides.

Slight pause.

NIKOLAI. What?

KELIMA. Diesel.

NIKOLAI. Diesel?

JAMES. Oh for Christ's sake . . .

FLOSS. Look do you mean / you won't –

KELIMA. I mean there is no point in medicine if no heat or light. So we cannot accept medical consignment.

JAMES. You can't *accept* it?

KELIMA. Luckily our generator run on diesel power. Presumably you must have diesel.

JAMES. So are you saying that you won't / accept the consignment –

FLOSS. James, it's clear enough what she's saying.

NIKOLAI. But I'm sorry this not possible.

KELIMA. Well it most clearly *possible* . . .

NIKOLAI. As last time we are let in diesel surprise surprise it is not use in hospital but for military purpose.

KELIMA (*to* FLOSS). This of course gross propaganda / and most typical –

NIKOLAI. No, gross propaganda is you move all patient to one hospital and invite on CNN. Gross propaganda is you fire big mortar round from hospital courtyard so returning fire seem like unprovoked attack on innocent civilian.

KELIMA. This quite typical as lies. You read it on their website.

NIKOLAI. Propaganda is when hospital / is use as front for –

JAMES. Can I just clear this up. You are saying you will not *receive* this medicine unless / the Kavkhazian army agrees –

FLOSS. Yes, James, that is what she means.

NIKOLAI. This is most typical of Drozhdan.

FLOSS (*to* JAMES). They're playing chicken.

NIKOLAI. So maybe now I say no deal? We keep your medicine?

FLOSS. You see?

KELIMA *gestures at the family.*

KELIMA. And we turn bus roundabout and drive off home. And tell Radio Liberty and BBC how much you care for your trapped people.

Pause.

NIKOLAI. OK. I call HQ.

He takes out his mobile phone.

KELIMA. Hey, you make long call on cellphone? Boy.

NIKOLAI. OK. I go use radio.

He makes to go as the 2nd KAVKHAZIAN SOLDIER *comes up to him with one of the IDs of the* FAMILY. *He takes him aside a little beyond* EMELA's *hearing.*

2nd KAVKHAZIAN (*Kavkhaz*). Goospoodín polkóvnik, sumnyávam se da li líchnata kárta e vuv ret. [Colonel, I'm a little worried about the ID.]

FLOSS (*to* KELIMA). He could use my handset.

NIKOLAI (*Kavkhaz*). Ne se beskpokóite. Shte gi proverím vednága. [Don't worry. We'll check them out. I want to sort this first.]

KELIMA (*gently*). No. It is better use his radio.

2nd KAVKHAZIAN (*Kavkhaz*). Slóusham goospoodíneh. [Yes, sir.]

NIKOLAI. OK.

NIKOLAI *goes out. The* 2nd KAVKHAZIAN SOLDIER *goes to talk to the family, waving the* 1st KAVKHAZIAN SOLDIER *to join him.*

2nd KAVKHAZIAN (*Kavkhaz*). Dragosláv, elá e pozdraví náshite rodníni. [Dragoslav. Come and welcome our cousins.]

KELIMA (*to* FLOSS). And maybe now you take my young friend Sergei to our fourwheel. He is very sick.

The BOY *doesn't look sick.*

FLOSS. He's sick?

KELIMA. Oh yes. Maybe kind UN man puts him in our fourwheel.

FLOSS. Why not.

She goes to LEN.

TREVELYAN. Why don't we take them all?

KELIMA. No, just the boy. I think we keep the others here.

En route to LEN, FLOSS *notices that the* KAVKHAZIAN SOLDIERS *are talking to the family and gestures* EMELA *to try and listen in. She goes over.* FLOSS *goes to the* UN SOLDIER. *NB: The dialogue between the* KAVKHAZIAN SOLIDERS *and the* FAMILY *is printed at the end of this scene.*

FLOSS. Len, can we put this young man in the cruiser?

LEN. Yes, sure thing.

LEN *goes over, takes the* BOY *by the hand.*

KELIMA. Uh, no, I mean our fourwheel.

FLOSS. Our landcruiser's better. It's got air-conditioning.

LEN *takes the* BOY *out.*

Right. We should call in to our HQ as well.

JAMES *reaches for his mobile,* FLOSS *shakes her head.*

JAMES. What, you want to leave the delivery unguarded?

FLOSS. Oh, why not. After all, it seems the least of anyone's concerns. Trev, go and marshall everyone.

TREVELYAN. Yuh. Sure.

He goes out. JAMES *looking bemused.* EMELA *comes forward.*

EMELA. Floss, one of the soldier speak to young man in wheelchair.

FLOSS. Yes?

EMELA. Soldier speak Kavkhazian.

FLOSS. Well they *are* Kavkhazian.

EMELA. I know. I just don't think they understand Kavkhazian completely well.

FLOSS. Oh, why?

EMELA. I not so up-to-speed on Kavkhaz slang. But I think soldier ask if he may fuck his mother.

They look over to the family just as the 2nd KAVKHAZIAN SOLDIER *draws his weapon. The* YOUNG MAN *stands up from the wheelchair with the pistol he has concealed underneath the blanket, and fires at the* 2nd KAVKHAZIAN SOLDIER, *who is shot and falls. The* 1st KAVKHAZIAN SOLDIER *ducks behind the supplies as the* FATHER *and* MOTHER *also produce weapons and fire.*

FLOSS. James! Emela! Get out!

FLOSS and EMELA run out the way NIKOLAI and LEN went out. The FAMILY opens fire on the consignment.

JAMES (*in despair*). Not the fucking supplies.

Blind, the 1st KAVKHAZIAN SOLDIER shoots JAMES and is shot himself. JAMES is wounded and falls. The 1st KAVKHAZIAN SOLDIER falls dead behind the supplies. KELIMA takes the FATHER's rifle and goes over to check that no one is returning.

KELIMA (*Drozhdani*). Hadi, chevik. [OK. Let's move, Quickly!]

The MOTHER and the YOUNG MAN move quickly to strip the KAVKHAZIAN SOLDIERS of their weapons and documents. The FATHER starts pulling out boxes from the cube. KELIMA to JAMES:

Are you OK?

JAMES. You fucking bastards. The *supplies*.

KELIMA. Where is the diamorphine?

JAMES. Surgical.

Sound of gunfire from off.

KELIMA (*Drozhdani*). Aman yarabbi, chevik ol! [Shit. Hurry!]

English, to JAMES:

And the valium?

JAMES. Diazepam. Basic Drugs kits.

KELIMA (*Drozhdani, calls*). Diyamorfini jarrahi baghlamalarda, diyazipamı uyushturujular paketlerinde tapajaksınız. [Find diamorphine in surgical kits, Diazepam in Basic Drugs.]

To JAMES:

Can I – is there anything to help?

JAMES. Well, I need something for the bleeding.

KELIMA. Uh . . .

She pulls her scarf off and uses it to wrap JAMES*'s arm.* JAMES *gestures to the* FATHER *who has taken a few kits from the cube.*

JAMES. And a jab. In fact, a little morphine wouldn't go amiss . . .

KELIMA (*Drozhdani, to the* FATHER). Diyamorfini tapın! [Find the diamorphine!]

The FATHER *searches as* KELIMA *continues to bind the wound.*

JAMES. There are no buses.

KELIMA. There are buses. There are no Kavkhazians.

JAMES. You could take it all.

KELIMA. We have no time.

JAMES. So you take the stuff that you can sell for arms.

KELIMA. Yes. This is a war you maybe notice.

JAMES. I notice you use kids to wage it.

KELIMA (*calls to the* FATHER, *in Drozhdani*). Paketi tap, chevik! [Find me the pack! Quickly!]

By now all the 'Kavkhazians' except the FATHER *are taking out boxes and running back for more. As the* FATHER *finds the surgical boxes and the morphine:*

KELIMA. Use kids as decoy. They use kids to kill.

JAMES. Oh, yuh?

KELIMA. Oh, yuh. Kids nine and ten are force to club own grandfather to death.

The FATHER *has the right pack. He is worried about the firing across his trajectory.*

JAMES. And so, what happened to the real family?

KELIMA *looks at* JAMES. *The* FATHER *calls.*

FATHER (*Drozhdani*). Hey, tutsana! [Hey! Catch!].

KELIMA *turns, the* FATHER *throws the pack, which* KELIMA *catches.*

JAMES. And for that matter, what will happen to the young boy now?

We hear the sound of helicopters. KELIMA *is tearing at the pack to get it open.*

KELIMA. Many time in war it does not always go as perfect plan.

YOUNG MAN (*Drozhdani, calls*). Helikopterlar galirlar ghaaliba. [I think that's helicopters].

KELIMA (*Drozhdani, calls*). Bali, hamla helikopterlar, kochun! [Yes, it's helicopter gunships! Move!]

JAMES. It's the blue one. Open it.

KELIMA. Helicopter come. You want we take you with us?

The FATHER *and* MOTHER *run out with the last of the packs. The* YOUNG MAN *stands, covering* KELIMA.

YOUNG MAN (*Drozhdani*). Hadi, galirlar! [Come on! They're coming in!]

JAMES. No. Just put it there, in my bad hand.

KELIMA. Now –

JAMES. I can do it with my good hand.

KELIMA. Now I have to go.

Calls, in Drozhdani:

San koch, man indi galiram! [Go! I'm coming!]

Helicopters louder. The YOUNG MAN *runs out.*

JAMES (*with the syringe*). I can't do this.

KELIMA *doesn't know what to do. She takes out her own mobile phone.*

KELIMA. Do you know his number? Shubkin's number?

JAMES. No. Did you call him earlier?

KELIMA. Last call.

She presses the callback number from the earlier call.

Kolya. You have a seriously wounded man here. No. No, we have gone. Trust me.

To JAMES*:*

Good luck.

She ends the call and runs out. The helicopters very loud, but the firing fades. JAMES *tries and fails to inject himself.* NIKOLAI *enters with his pistol and the* BOY *as a human shield.*

NIKOLAI. They are gone?

JAMES. Yes.

NIKOLAI. They leave supply.

JAMES. They leave supply. Look, I . . .

Enter FLOSS.

FLOSS. Oh my God.

NIKOLAI. Oh my God yes very much.

NIKOLAI *is pointing his pistol at* FLOSS.

FLOSS. I'm – this is terrible.

NIKOLAI. Yes, this is terrible.

JAMES. Floss I need this jab. As a matter of some urgency.

FLOSS (*to* NIKOLAI). I need / to help –

NIKOLAI. Do not Miss Florence Hazel Weatherby please take one step towards that man.

FLOSS. Why not?

NIKOLAI. Miss Weatherby you are entrust with UN mandate.

FLOSS. Yes. But first I am entrusted with / the lives and safety –

NIKOLAI. Provide humanitarian assistance. Keep security and safety for all citizen.

FLOSS *sees that* JAMES *is fainting.*

FLOSS. Colonel Shubkin, I must help my colleague.

NIKOLAI. Yes, but first you must help me. As you see I trust
   your friends and now my friends are dead. No safety no
   security for them. And being naturally a primitive barbarian /
   I naturally –

FLOSS. Oh, Kolya, please . . .

NIKOLAI. I naturally believe in Bible, taking tooth for tooth
   and eye for eye. So which I kill. This boy or else your
   friend.

FLOSS. What do you mean?

NIKOLAI. One must be kill. Your call.

FLOSS. My *call*?

NIKOLAI. Your friend or this little man who maybe you think
   you are here to save. You choose. Your call.

FLOSS. This isn't serious.

NIKOLAI. I seem not serious?

FLOSS. Then OK. Shoot me.

NIKOLAI. No, not an option. Choose.

   Pause.

FLOSS. Look. Look, demonstrably –

   NIKOLAI *shoots the* BOY.

   Oh God.

   She realises:

   No, don't –

   NIKOLAI *shoots* JAMES. FLOSS *closes her eyes.*

NIKOLAI. You see. You may save one. But you refuse. If you
   will choose one, one will be now alive. But you cannot
   choose.

   A mobile phone rings. It's JAMES*'s mobile.* NIKOLAI *goes
   and answers it.*

Hallo? No, this is not James Neil. What must you say for him?

Pause.

Thank you. Well no, I'm sorry. Mr Neil is dead. I have just kill him.

He switches off the phone.

You go home now. UN declare evacuation of all NGOs. You go, they bomb.

He tosses her JAMES*'s phone.*

I think it better. This place not for you. 'Demonstrably'.

He turns and goes out. FLOSS *goes to the* BOY, *then to* JAMES, *to check they're dead. As she does she repeats the ground rules of the operation.*

FLOSS. When approaching checkpoints, always turn off radio and headlamps, turn on cabin lights. Check everyone aware of current evacuation plan. Check waybill, packing list and clearances for each stop at each stop. Do not forget the emergency radio codeword. All non essential traffic must stop when this word is used. The code is 'Gameshow'.

A helicopter above. FLOSS *looks up.*

Appendix for Scene One

Dialogue for KAVKHAZIAN SOLDIERS *and the* FAMILY *on page 90.*

2nd KAVKHAZIAN (*Kavkhaz*). E, kák si? Kak putóova? [So how are you? You have good journey?]

MOTHER (*Kavkhaz, not very assured*). Putóovakh me dobré. [Yes, we have good journey.]

2nd KAVKHAZIAN (*Kavkhaz*). Bíkha li vi mútri? [Did the bandits beat you up?]

FATHER (*Kavkhaz*). Ne. Ne ni bíkha. [No, they do not beat us up.]

1st KAVKHAZIAN (*Kavkhaz*). Ochúdvashto. Míslekh che vi bíyat, shte vi otkrádnat bagázha. [That's a surprise. I'd expect they'd beat you up and steal your property.]

YOUNG MAN (*Kavkhaz*). Te ni otkrádnakha bagázha. [Well, they do steal our property.]

FATHER (*Kavkhaz*). Govédo. [The bastards.]

2nd KAVKHAZIAN (*Kavkhaz*). Ni tryábva da vi namérim dóbro mýasto za otsýadane sus náshite khora. [We will have to find a good place for you to stay among your own people.]

MOTHER (*Kavkhaz*). Da. [Yes.]

FATHER (*Kavkhaz*). Da, tuk e lóssho mýasto. [Yes it is not a good place.]

1st KAVKHAZIAN (*Kavkhaz*). Ti rodén li si i izrásnal vuf Estafán? [So were you born and bred in Estafan?]

YOUNG MAN (*Kavkhaz*). Mólya? [I'm sorry?]

1st KAVKHAZIAN (*Kavkhaz*). Az te pítam, rodén li si i izrásnal vuf Estafán? [I ask you if you were born and bred in Estafan?]

YOUNG MAN (*Kavkhaz*). Da. Az sum rodén i izrásnal vuf Estafan. [Yes, I was born and bred in Estafan.]

FATHER (*Kavkhaz*). Ni sme vsíchki ot Estafán. [We are all from Estafan.]

2nd KAVKHAZIAN (*Kavkhaz*). Togáva da te zapítam droógo néshto. Kak shte se pochústvash, áko az shte raspórya ot ébane táya zhená? [Let me ask another question. How would you feel if I was to have a Number 10 shag with this woman here?]

YOUNG MAN (*Kavkhaz*). Ti pítash, koyá e tázi zhená? [You ask me who is this woman here?]

1st KAVKHAZIAN (*Kavkhaz*). Smýatash li che tová mu béshe vuprósut? [You think that was his question?]

YOUNG MAN (*Kavkhaz*). Tázi zhená e máika mi. [This woman is my mother.]

Scene Two

Four months later. The helicopter lands. The deck of a US warship in the Eastern Mediterranean. There is a searail and a bench. GINA *walks on, carrying her briefcase, her suitcase carried by a woman* SAILOR *from the US Navy.*

GINA. So do I meet Professor Rothman and Mr Davis now?

SAILOR. Excuse me?

GINA. Professor Rothman of the . . . US State Department?

SAILOR. I regret ma'am I am not aware of Professor Rothman's schedule at this time.

A frisbee – marked 'Property of the US Navy' – flies in at GINA. *She catches it.*

GINA. Um, I . . .

A BODYGUARD *enters, followed by an older* MAN *in tennis clothes. The* SAILOR *comes to attention. The* MAN *is* YURI VASILEVICH PETROVIAN, *President of the Republic of Kavkhazia.*

YURI VASILEVICH. I am so sorry. Only in Kavkhazia. The Presidential Bodyguard, this terrible a shot.

GINA (*what to do with the frisbee*). Um . . .

YURI VASILEVICH. Thank you.

The BODYGUARD *does to 'to me' gesture, and* GINA *tosses him the frisbee, which he catches with some aplomb.* YURI YASILEVICH *gestures that he may go and he does.*

YURI VASILEVICH (*to the* SAILOR). Thank you so much.

The SAILOR *looks to* GINA.

GINA. Yes, thank you.

The SAILOR *puts down* GINA's *bag and goes.*

YURI VASILEVICH. So welcome to USS Idaho, currently I understand precisely equidistant between Karpathos and Crete. My name is Yuri Vasilevich Petrovian. I am General Secretary of the Democratic Socialist Alliance Party of Kavkhazia and President of the Republic.

He puts out his hand.

GINA. Yes, I know. I'm Gina Olsson.

She shakes his hand.

YURI VASILEVICH. Ah yes. The sadly only yet so nearly but so far Agreement of Geneva. Well now we may shake our hands at last.

GINA. Very sadly in my view.

YURI VASILEVICH. It was not yet his time.

GINA. After so many unnecessary deaths, maybe now will be its time. When the game is no longer about who wins, so both sides may.

YURI VASILEVICH. Like playing frisbee.

Enter PATTERSON, *on crutches, and* TOM ROTHMAN, *now in his late 50s.*

Ah. The 'Men in Black'.

GINA *looks questioningly.*

There is a white one and a coloured one. They possess considerable you might say extravagant fire-power. They think anyone who is not American is from another planet.

Louder:

I am with you Miss Olsson. I think we should play both side wins. But sadly, each time we send over frisbee, our opponents send back discus. Mr Davis, Mr Rothman, please forgive me. I have appointment to play squash with your chief military attaché.

He gives a little bow to PATTERSON *and* ROTHMAN, *and turns to go.*

TOM. Well, good luck, Mr President.

YURI VASILEVICH *goes out, as* PATTERSON *whips out a notebook, writing something down before he forgets it.* TOM *comes over to* GINA.

GINA. Well, Professor Rothman.

TOM (*shaking her hand*). Technically, Mr Special Representative. Actually, Tom. I'm delighted you could make it.

PATTERSON *puts away his notebook, hobbles over.*

GINA. Well, Patterson.

PATTERSON (*coming over*). So hey Gina Olsson and how's stuff with *you*?

They embrace, with a little difficulty.

GINA. I am very well. One question.

PATTERSON. I may never rollerblade again.

GINA. No, I actually meant, what you were writing down.

PATTERSON. 'We sent a frisbee, they send back a discus'.

TOM. We're collecting suspect analogies.

GINA. I beg your pardon?

PATTERSON (*reading from his little book*). 'To put the DPF in charge of the security of Kavkhazian religious sites is like employing Adolf Hitler to organise your son's bar mitzvah'.

TOM. Taste not being the strong point of the genre.

GINA. Though in this case he is presumably quite right.

Slight pause.

TOM. Yes, almost certainly.

PATTERSON. Hey, now, would you like to freshen up?

GINA. I'd like to know what you require of me. The last time I intervened in the affairs of the Kavkhazian\Drozhdan region it led to civil war.

TOM. Now, Gina, that's ridiculous.

GINA. Oh you think so?

TOM. Or else why would we deny the students and faculty of the Sorbonne your expertise and wisdom, and drag you here?

GINA *sits on the bench, opening her briefcase, and taking out papers and faxes.*

GINA. Yes, my next question.

PATTERSON *and* TOM *sit either side of her.*

TOM. Summarize the current Kavkhazian position, as you see it.

GINA. What, from the files?

PATTERSON. That's right.

GINA *is slightly discommoded by what seems to be a test.*

GINA. I only got these on the plane.

Slight pause.

OK. Well, thanks to your bombing threat, they've actually come on quite considerably since Finland. They are offering pretty much everything except for independence.

TOM. In exchange for?

GINA. Well, essentially, protection of the security and safety of the Kavkhazian minority . . . language, religious sites and cemeteries . . .

TOM. But, crucially?

GINA. Well, crucially, they are insisting that the Kavkhars have the power of veto over major issues in the regional assembly.

TOM. Like?

GINA. Well, for a start, control of policing and the justice system, pretty vitally I'd say . . .

PATTERSON. Geneva Lesson One.

TOM. And after two years of a bitter civil war.

GINA. But I would imagine not so popular with the Drozhdanis. And as you got everybody here by threatening to bomb Kavkhazia, the Drozhdans must assume that if they hang on long enough, then you'll have to carry out your threat.

TOM. Sure.

GINA. And the Kavkhazians presumably assume you'd never do it.

TOM. Right.

GINA. So then, in answer to my question?

GINA *shuts her case.*

PATTERSON. The United States remains committed to the achievement of a peaceful, multi-ethnic, democratic future for all peoples of the Bela river basin. It does not believe it could persuade the Kavkhaz Government nor its allies nor indeed the world community that independence for Drozhdania provides a context for that aim to be achieved.

GINA. By which you mean you can't persuade the Russians to accept it.

TOM. Well, Kavkhazia is a former Soviet Republic.

PATTERSON. So in answer to your question, what we want of you is to persuade the Drozhdans of the virtue and good sense of doing what is in their ultimate best interests. And thus to finish up on what you started so propitiously at Outokumpu.

GINA. And what makes you think that I'd do any better than I did last time?

TOM. OK. We know what people say about backchannels. What happens is, you bring the guys together who are likely to discover that they share a passion for fly-fishing, bordeaux wine or the novels of Jane Austen, and darn it you exclude and thereby stiffen up the spoilers on both sides. And there's an argument that those other guys have stuff in common too, not least an inclination towards lopping off each other's heads and sticking them on poles. And we fear it may be actually *because* they know each other that they act this way. You know, just like those scenes in Shakespeare plays where guys called towns turn out to be first cousins married to each other's sisters and no wonder they all end up knee deep in each other's gore.

Pause.

But surely we don't want to think that, do we? Surely we can't believe that on the edge of Europe at the beginning of the new millennium it's impossible for people from a different ethnic origin to live together in some kind of amity? If that was true, how could we live with it?

Pause.

GINA. So the two sides are . . . completely separate?

TOM. With precedents which stretch back to the treaty of Westphalia.

PATTERSON. And if they don't sign up to something, here, in two days' time, then all bets are off, and everyone goes home.

GINA. So there's no . . . they can't take a document back to ratify?

TOM. No.

PATTERSON. Geneva, Lesson Two.

GINA. And the delegations are supported from outside?

TOM. Yes, but in situ.

PATTERSON. No calling home.

TOM. No mobile phones.

PATTERSON. The Drozhdans have a former Presidential special counsel.

TOM. Very former. And not very special.

PATTERSON. And there's a guy here who you know.

GINA *looks enquiringly.*

TOM. Bit of a smartass.

PATTERSON. Kavkhaz origin, in fact.

TOM. Hawaiian shirt.

PATTERSON. Al Bek.

Slight pause.

GINA. Ah.

TOM. It was him who started the analogy collection.

GINA. Was it now. He's with the Drozhdan delegation also?

TOM. No. He's with the bad guys.

GINA. Bad guys.

TOM. And I can't believe I said that, Pat, can you?

Slight pause.

And nor can I believe I'm going to say the following, but it's the truth. You're here because two people who sincerely want to stop this nightmare feel – but cannot say – that the good guys seem at present neither smart enough nor nice enough to help.

He sees someone approaching.

I'll see you later.

He goes out. KELIMA *enters, to lean on the rail and smoke a cigarette.*

PATTERSON (*to* GINA). It wasn't wrong in principle. It was the wrong time. There is a season for all things under heaven. And we have to think, now, that the time is ripe to make a little history.

KELIMA *looks over and sees* GINA.

Of course you know Kelima Bejta. Who like every member of the Drozhdan delegation has the right of veto over all decisions. They call it 'decision-making by consensus'. We call it something else.

PATTERSON *goes out.*

GINA. Hallo.

KELIMA. I hear that you are coming.

GINA. Well, and here I am.

KELIMA. You are no longer in diplomacy?

GINA. No. I am in academia.

Slight pause.

Hasim Majdani's here?

KELIMA. He is. In fact now he high leadership.

GINA. So I understand. I'm pleased. So how / are the talks –

KELIMA. I think you know of Florence Weatherby.

GINA. Why do you mention her?

KELIMA. I see her recently.

GINA. Yes, so I heard.

KELIMA. Where we both learn that what you choose to say and do in a midst of civil war can be a matter of some consequence.

GINA. Of course. I understand that. Which is why I'm here.

KELIMA. Me also.

GINA. And because I promised you Geneva wouldn't be the end.

KELIMA. So once again we play game 'what is other person thinking'. And pray this time you get it right.

KELIMA *turns and goes quickly out.* GINA *picks up her suitcase and goes out the other way.*

Scene Three

*The next day. Night. The stateroom in which the Drozhdan
delegation meets. Papers on a large table. Somewhere there
might be an updated ethnic map of Kavkhazia, with hatched-in,
mixed areas much smaller than when we last saw the map, and
the exclusively Kavkhar and Drozhdani areas much larger. AL
BEK, now 38, sits with his feet up on the table. GINA enters
with her briefcase and documents. She is surprised and not
pleased to see AL.*

GINA. Ah.

AL. Hey, Mohammad? Mountain.

GINA. I beg your pardon?

AL. After all, it's been all of a whole day.

GINA. The meeting starts here shortly.

AL. The meeting starts here a quarter of an hour ago. But then,
    it's a meeting of the Drozhdan delegation.

GINA. I think you'll find tonight it will start shortly. There is
    much to do.

AL. What, like rubberstamp the terms for our surrender?

GINA. No, to find your next and better option.

AL. Oh, yuh, that old thing.

GINA. I was surprised . . . I thought you were inclined towards
    your father's side.

AL. Hey, listen. I'm a lawyer. I'm a cab. You hire me, and tell
    me where you want to go.

GINA. What, they hail you first?

AL. Also I married a Kavkhaz girl.

    Slight pause.

GINA. Aha.

AL. How's . . . Erik? And, uh, Jan?

GINA. Well done. Oh, Erik is just fine. He sees more of Jan than I do, in the term time, as he lives nearby Jan's school.

AL. Aha.

GINA. And that's when I'm not in France.

AL. Oho.

GINA. And what does this, this 'Kavkhaz girl' tell you that you didn't know about your roots?

AL. A people which comes into a barren place and makes it grow. A country which is invaded and defeated and enslaved, more times that it cares to count. Which stands up when it can to outside force on behalf of, yes, actually, European values, culture, civilisation, and where it can't, which tries to keep that dream alive. And when at last it wins the right to run its own affairs, in its own way, the world turns round and calls it a pariah. And indeed claims that it stands, not for culture and enlightenment, but mediaeval barbarism. And tries to expel it from that very company of nations it has stood on Europe's outer ramparts to defend.

GINA. There is . . . is there not, something perhaps a little bit intoxicating about that story.

AL. There's something perhaps a little bit tragic / about it –

GINA. All that loss. So many times, to stand up so alone, defiant yet defeated. But actually *everybody* thinks they are the last bulwark against the bestial hordes. Everybody thinks: beyond us, the barbarians.

AL. Especially the Finns.

GINA. Of course. Whereas in fact / if you look just to the east of Finland –

AL. Whereas in fact the Drozhdans are actually the epitome of civilised contemporary values. As they put it, if the choice is coca cola or cyrillic, we choose coke. If it's country music or the balalaika, we'll go for Nashville every time. In fact, you could say that the Drozhdan way is US capitalism, red in tooth and claw. Strange bedfellows for you.

GINA. They're not my bedfellows.

AL. No, sure. The honest broker.

GINA. And if they are so familiar with the market system, then surely it's because they were excluded from the state one for so long.

AL. That and the fact the marketplace is where you find narcotics, arms and girls.

Slight pause.

GINA. I'm sorry, but we should not have this conversation.

AL. I'm sorry also, but not just for that.

Slight pause.

GINA. Yes, what?

AL. I gather you've been helping them to, what? – to 'focus' their demands.

GINA. I've been trying to help them put together something both sides can accept.

AL. Oh then I've got it wrong. I thought it was a test designed for us to fail.

GINA. So why would anybody set a test for you to fail?

AL. Easy. If what you really want isn't spending five years policing an agreement, but five weeks or five days humiliating the Kavkhazians sufficiently for them to rise and overthrow their President.

GINA. Well, good.

AL. Why good?

GINA. Because Petrovian's a war criminal.

AL. No more than half the leaders of the world.

GINA. I would contest that.

AL. Sure. But what you can't contest is that the US has another interest in getting rid of him.

GINA. Go on.

AL. Has anybody talked about the economics of this thing to you?

GINA. What, the west wants to get its hands on a clapped-out nickel mine, some superannuated smelting plants and a mountain-full of ecologically lethal Drozhdanian brown coal?

AL. Well, don't underestimate the nickel or the coal. The world needs batteries. Drozhdevnyan power stations supply half of southern Russia.

GINA. Good for southern Russia.

AL. But the real issue is the oil.

GINA. Neither Drozhdania nor Kavkhazia have any oil.

AL. I am talking naturally about the pipeline from the Caspian which as you'll know can either run through an increasingly Islamic and anti-US Gezekhstan or through Kavkhazia and western Drozdhevnya to the sea.

GINA. I'm sorry, I'm not one for sinister conspiracies.

AL. But, Gina, you're the victim of a sinister conspiracy. Don't you understand? They've brought you here to fail. So they can say, hey, look, we did our best, we went that extra mile, hell, we even jetted in some crazy lefty Nordic feminist to have them all hear inner voices and do drums, but still the bastard wouldn't budge. And so eventually, reluctantly, they impose a US-friendly independent Drozhdan state on us from 15,000 feet.

Pause.

GINA. If that's the case, then there's an easy way to stop it.

AL. Oh?

GINA. Accept the deal.

AL. As I say, it's designed for us to fail.

GINA. I don't agree.

AL. Ask yourself: What is the one thing on the table we could never give away.

PATTERSON *enters, now with one crutch, and papers.*

PATTERSON. Hi, Al.

AL. Hi, Pat.

PATTERSON. Hey, isn't this the stateroom of the Drozhdan delegation?

AL. Sure.

To GINA*:*

What happens is that you put two sets of people with two options in two rooms. And you have some smart guys running back and forth from room to room telling one thing to one group and another to the other. But I'm told there is one question you can ask, to find out if they're telling you the truth.

GINA. Yes. 'Sure'. I remember.

AL. As, of course, the liar lies about the fact he'd lie.

AL *goes out.* PATTERSON *gets himself to the table.*

PATTERSON. So what's the scoop?

GINA. They've not decided.

PATTERSON. I hope you underlined the overwhelming argument for swerving.

GINA. Is that really what you wanted me to do?

PATTERSON. Of course.

PATTERSON *sees the Drozhdan delegation entering.*

I'll lead this one, OK?

Enter the Drozhdan delegation, which includes KELIMA, HASIM MAJDANI, *the 31-year-old military leader* ZELIM ZAGAYEV, *his translator* EMELA, *and* LOU WASSERMAN, *an American lawyer in his early 50s.*

HASIM. Good evening.

LOU. Hi, Pat.

PATTERSON. Hey everybody's here. Miss Olsson, I told you. You gotta have a little faith in people.

GINA smiles wanly. She and PATTERSON sit, followed by the others.

LOU. Yuh, sorry. We are fourteen minutes late.

PATTERSON. There speaks a former counsel to the United Auto Workers. And we were a tad late too. But at least, for all of us, that concentrates the mind.

This statement concentrates everybody's mind.

For very shortly I have to take a call from a Most Important Person and I'd really like to tell him we're approaching closure here.

EMELA is whispering the translation to ZELIM:

EMELA (*Drozhdani, to* ZELIM). Chokh mühüm bir kishi zang edajaq ona. [He has a call coming in from a VIP.]

LOU. And what Most Important Person might that be?

PATTERSON. Well, I think you've met him, Lou. As I recollect, you've got a picture of him standing with you on the sidewalk just outside the Waldorf on your wall.

LOU. The President.

ZELIM (*to* EMELA). Petrovian?

EMELA (*on* ZELIM's *behalf*). This is President of Kavkhazia?

PATTERSON. No, the president of the United States. Who calls at 4.00pm Eastern Standard Time and to whom I intend to give an answer. The President of Kavkhazia is resident, and we can consult at any time.

KELIMA stands, goes and gets an empty chair, places it at the table and sits back in her own chair.

What's this?

HASIM. Ms Olsson think it good for us to have empty chair at table, representing President Petrovian.

PATTERSON. Ms Olsson is surely right. However, at this moment, I would like you to consider this.

He pushes the documents round the table so EVERYONE *can take one.*

EMELA. What is this?

PATTERSON. It's the latest draft of the agreement.

EMELA. And you like for us to consider this.

PATTERSON. Consider and agree.

Pause.

HASIM. This evening.

PATTERSON. This hour.

Pause.

EMELA (*Drozhdani, to* ZELIM). Bu yeni musvadda'yi bir saat ichariya kaabul etmamiz laazımdır. [This is the new draft for us to agree within an hour.]

LOU. It will be hard to do that unless it is substantially different from the previous document.

PATTERSON. OK. It is different in that we have firmed up – at your insistence – the position of the Drozhdan language not only in schools but in all official communications and government departments.

This line as PATTERSON *goes on:*

EMELA (*Drozhdani, to* ZELIM). Drozhdan dil shartları sübütlandı. [The Drozdhan language provisions are firmed up.]

PATTERSON. And it is different – crucially – in that in the spirit of democracy and equal rights for all, there is no longer a Kavkhaz veto on anything in the assembly, including matters relating to government employment, education, health provision and security.

EMELA (*Drozhdani, to* ZELIM). Kavkhaz vetoso qaldırıldı.

[And they've removed the Kavkhaz veto.]

GINA. I'm sorry?

PATTERSON. It is different, crucially, in that in the context of democracy and equal / rights for all –

GINA. No, I heard.

PATTERSON. I'm glad, because it's what this delegation has demanded. Constantly.

GINA. But surely/, it's impossible –

HASIM. But surely it no different in that it will not offer us independent Drozhdania.

EMELA (*Drozhdani, to* ZELIM). Majdaani bunun farq etmayajaini deyir. [Majdani says it is no different.]

ZELIM (*Drozhdani*). Ona de ki Majdaani haqlıdır. [Tell him Madjani's right].

PATTERSON. No. It offers a degree – a huge degree, much greater than before – of sovereignty and autonomy. But no, not independence.

EMELA. So, Commander Zagayev says, it is not different at all.

PATTERSON. It's the same in that it denies you the right to join another state.

Impatience.

But as you have all said repeatedly that you don't wish to join another state I can't see that's a problem.

This line underneath the following two lines:

EMELA (*Drozhdani, to* ZELIM). Gezekhstanla birlashmak istamassaq problem olmayajaq deyir. [He says it's no problem unless we want to join Gezekhstan.]

LOU. Pat, that's like saying if you don't want to travel it doesn't matter if they take away your passport.

PATTERSON. No, it isn't, Lou, that's frankly a ridiculous analogy \ and you know it –

GINA. The final difference being that it is considered by the Kavkhazian delegation as we speak.

Pause.

PATTERSON. As Ms Olsson reminds me, helpfully.

EMELA. You mean, they consider now this document?

PATTERSON. That's right.

HASIM. And will they accept it?

PATTERSON. I have no idea.

EMELA (*Drozhdani, to* ZELIM). Deyir ki Kavkharlar musvadda'yi indi teemmül edayirlar. [She says the Kavkhars are considering this now.]

KELIMA. And will they know what we decide before they do?

Slight pause.

PATTERSON. No they will not. And visa-versa, obviously.

Pause.

KELIMA. So it is possible that neither will accept this document.

PATTERSON. Clearly.

LOU. In which case, all the acronyms go home.

PATTERSON. As night follows day.

EMELA (*Drozhdani, to* ZELIM). Agar iki taraf kaabul etmassa, USA, UN va NATO gari chakajaqlar. [If neither side accepts this, the USA, UN and NATO withdraw.]

KELIMA. But it also possible for both accept. In / which case –

PATTERSON. – in which case an excellent agreement will be implemented.

No one is entirely convinced.

EMELA (*Drozhdani, to* ZELIM). Iki taraf iyi sazish kaabul edajaq. [Both sides accept a good agreement.]

PATTERSON. And obviously in theory you could say no and they could say yes.

KELIMA. But the possibility to be considered most actually presumably is not that but the opposite. We agree and they will not.

PATTERSON. That would appear to follow.

KELIMA. And hi there B52s. And farewell President Petrovian.

Pause.

PATTERSON. As I say, we wish both sides to go for this. But if they don't, and you do, then they will have to think about the consequences.

GINA *stands, goes round to 'Petrovian's' chair, and sits in it.*

PATTERSON. Yes, Gina?

GINA. I've a question.

PATTERSON. Mr President.

GINA. If I asked you what the hell you're trying to make me do, what would you say?

But YURI VASILEVICH *is already in the room, followed by* ROMAN *and a troubled* TOM. GINA *rises.*

YURI VASILEVICH. Well good evening Mr Patterson Davis, and distinguished members of Drozhdani delegation. Miss Olsson please do not get up.

PATTERSON. Mr President?

YURI VASILEVICH. Now is this my chair?

GINA *sits.* YURI VASILEVICH *sits in what was* GINA*'s chair.* PATTERSON *looks at* TOM, *who answers the implied question with a gesture halfway between a shake and a shrug.*

Now in handbook the first thing they say is that the point of talks like these is *not* for door she suddenly fly open and behold the other side walk in the room and everything is

solve. The idea indeed is quite exactly that communication
goes via these good people and so to speak the medium is
the messenger. Certainly this was the way of things at the
Treaty of Westphalia.

He picks up a biscuit and tastes it, as:

EMELA (*Drozhdani, to* ZELIM). Iki taraf bashbasha danıshmalı
deyir. [He says that the two sides should speak directly.]

YURI VASILEVICH. Ah you have cookies. We have cheese.
When we begin, stupendous choice. Now there is only one.
But I am assured it is the best.

EMELA (*Drozhdani, to* ZELIM). Biskuvit haqqında zeraafet
eder. [He jokes about the biscuits.]

YURI VASILEVICH (*standing and going round the table*).
But why should I not talk direct with Commander Zagayev,
who come here from his job as public gardener in Munich
to lead great freedom-loving private army?

EMELA (*Drozhdani, to* ZELIM). Sizi hamla edir, ve indi mani
hamla edajaq. [He is attacking you. And I think now me.]

YURI VASILEVICH. With his beautiful translator with her
perfect Kavkhaz and Gezhekh, oh I am so sorry Kavkhaz
and 'Drozhdanian', why should we have to talk via the
diplomatic corps of the United States?

EMELA (*Drozhdani, to* ZELIM). Dediyim kimi. [As I say.]

YURI VASILEVICH. Why should I not have chat with my old
friend and comrade Dr Hasim Majdani. We share many
memories. Not like these bright young people for whom
epoch of socialism like mediaeval times. We know about all
Russian yoke.

EMELA (*Drozhdani, to* ZELIM). Sosialist era haqqında
danıshır. [He talks about socialist days.]

YURI VASILEVICH. And yeah sure they are United States.
If they tell us Monday's Tuesday then we must nod politely
and agree. But secretly we whisper. Wednesday is today.
Knowing that there is nothing in United States as old or
maybe we might think as beautiful as one solitary orchard
in Kavkhazia.

EMELA (*Drozhdani, to* ZELIM). Kavkhazyadaki eski baghlar haqqında hissi danıshma [Sentiment about old orchards in Kavkhazia.]

Enter AL *with a pile of papers.*

YURI VASILEVICH. And I see Mr Wasserman.

Corrects himself elaborately:

I beg his pardon *Counsel* Wasserman. But see. I have my Counsel too.

He takes the documents from AL*:*

We word process. Nice clean copy. I am told the crucial thing in these negotiations is to understand the real interests of both side.

EMELA (*Drozhdani, to* ZELIM). Yeni bir sanad. [It's a new document.]

He distributes the documents:

YURI VASILEVICH. We want to stay one country. They want to be a country too. Maybe you expect for me to bring a sword or ploughshare but I bring something else. A pair of – how d'you say it?

He mimes scissors.

TOM. Scissors.

YURI VASILEVICH. Scissors.

EMELA (*Drozhdani, to* ZELIM). Qaychı haqqında bir shey danıshır. [It's something about scissors.]

YURI VASILEVICH (*to* PATTERSON). You should write that down.

He goes out.

PATTERSON (*to* TOM). What is it?

TOM (*to* PATTERSON). Well, you could say, they've changed their next best option. And thereby everybody else's. And thereby, the game.

EMELA (*Drozhdani, to* ZELIM). Yepyeni bir oyun. [A whole new game.]

ROMAN *sits.*

ROMAN. We are trying to address the problem of two opposites that seem irreconcilable. Our proposal has an ancient precedent. It is based on a Talmudic principle: 'Where justice prevails, there is not peace, and where peace prevails there is no justice. So where is the justice that contains peace? Indeed it is in partition'.

EMELA (*Drozhdani, to* ZELIM). Hududu dayıshtırmak istayirlar. [They are proposing to redraw the border.]

ZELIM (*Drozhdani*). Na? [What?]

ROMAN (*referring to his copy of the document*). The new border remains open to negotiation. The Bela river forms a natural boundary for a proportion of its length.

EMELA (*Drozhdani, to* ZELIM). Hududu, chay boyuna chizdilar. [They have redrawn the border along the river.]

ROMAN. We have drawn it obviously with our population and religious sites on our side. Some people perhaps will wish and need to leave their homes but we hope not too many.

EMELA (*Drozhdani, to* ZELIM). Milli tamizlama olajaq laakin az olajaqtır. [There will be ethnic cleansing but not too much.]

He looks round the table.

AL. In fact there's some US Air Force software we've been playing with, which effectively maps the territory in 3-D. You see it as if you're flying over in an airplane. So you get a sense of natural defences, mountains, rivers and the like.

ROMAN. And therefore what's defensible against a neighbour. On the principle good neighbours need good walls. So maybe you need time to read this document?

These next two lines underneath the following six:

EMELA (*Drozhdani, to* ZELIM). Onu bilgisayarda chizdilar. Sanadi okhumayi istarik mi? [They have worked it out on a computer. Do we want to read the document?]

ZELIM (*Drozhdani*). Kishidan Berushka nikeli va Agaridaki madeni tasfiyakhaanalar haqqında sor. [Ask him about the Berushka nickel and the smelting plants in Agari.]

HASIM. So new Drozhdania is independent?

AL. No more or less than the United States.

HASIM. And is Estafan in Drozhdania?

ROMAN. Of course. It is a Muslim town.

LOU. And Bazarat?

ROMAN. The majority of the population of the town of Basda Brod lives on the west bank of the Bela river.

KELIMA *looks up and then back to the document, as:*

EMELA. Commander Zagayev asks about Berushka nickel mine and the Atagi smelting plants.

AL. And the answer is, that the Berushka coal field – and the nickel mines – stay in Drozhdania. Atagi on the other hand is a centre of Kavkhaz population and indeed religious sites. But all of this is subject / to negotiation –

GINA. I'm sorry, I . . . This is quite abject. This is a betrayal. Worse, this is surrender.

ROMAN. Of what? By who?

GINA. Of the spirit of a peaceful democratic multi-ethnic state with equal rights for all.

Pause.

HASIM (*referring to the document*). Whereas, instead, what we are offered is two states in which the population may be ruled 'by those to whom they feel historical affinity'.

GINA. Achieved by dumping all the bits they don't want and keeping all the bits they do.

HASIM. We keep the nickel and the coal.

GINA. But they get the smelting plants and power stations?

HASIM. So we must trade.

GINA. Oh, sure. And what d'you make of 'some people will wish and need to leave their homes'?

ROMAN. However you redraw the map, there will be mixed areas.

GINA. No, I want to hear what *he* thinks.

PATTERSON. Gina . . .

HASIM. Wherever you draw border there are mixed areas.

GINA points to the updated ethnic map.

GINA. But not of course so many as there were two years ago. But more now than in two years time. If there are any left at all.

To ROMAN*:*

What did we say? That whether it's a country or a region, no one thinks it would be right or even possible to split it into two.

TOm. Look, I'm afraid / we need to reach –

GINA (*to* ROMAN, *then to* HASIM). 'Of course'. 'Look at the map'. But I guess that that was then and this is now.

TOM. Look, I'm sorry, but in view of an imminent communcation, time is pressing down on us.

KELIMA. Oh I hardly think so Mr Rothman.

PATTERSON (*glance at watch*). Well, in fact . . .

KELIMA. Because there will be nothing to communicate.

Slight pause.

ROMAN. Um, why . . .

KELIMA. As I do not sign this document.

She stands.

'Decision making by consensus'. As he call it, something else.

KELIMA *goes out.*

LOU. What happens now?

TOM. What happens is we take five. Gina.

GINA. Yes of course.

> GINA, TOM *and* PATTERSON *go out on to the deck. The others are left there.*

ZELIM (*Drozhdani*). Yoldash Bejta haraya getti? [Where did Comrade Bejta go?]

EMELA (*Drozhdani, to* ZELIM). Sazishi veto etti ghaaliba. [I think she has vetoed the agreement.]

> ZELIM *stands to go after.* HASIM *stands too.*

ZELIM (*Drozhdani*). Man gedip danışıram onla. [I will go and speak with her.]

HASIM. We go and speak together.

ROMAN. No in fact this is not such a good idea.

HASIM. Why?

ZELIM (*Drozhdani*). Na deyir? [What is he saying?]

ROMAN. As Dr Majdani is well aware, we have been here before.

Scene Four

Continuous. Night. GINA, TOM *and* PATTERSON *on the upper deck.*

TOM. Or put another way, what happens is that you persuade Ms Bejta to withdraw her veto.

GINA. Oh, why?

PATTERSON. Because it's what they want.

GINA. It's clearly what Majdani wants. To see his face on all the stamps. To review the march past of the palace guard.

PATTERSON. And that's so bad?

GINA. It clearly isn't good enough for her.

TOM. Nor you. Which is why, right now, you're the only
person who can talk to her.

GINA. So I wonder why it's good enough for you?

GINA *goes down to the lower deck.* ROMAN *and*
PATTERSON *follow.*

PATTERSON. Well, because it will make peace. The traditional
purpose of diplomacy.

GINA. Yuh. And you get to lift the sanctions and you get your
pipeline and your client state . . .

TOM. Gina, if this was all about a goddam pipeline we'd be
dancing round the deck.

GINA. But in fact I don't think it's about these things at all.
It's not even about punishing the Kavkhars for making you
look stupid at Geneva or overthrowing President Petrovian.
I think it's really just so you can say: 'We are Americans.
We want a world where everyone will live together, across
the ethnic divide, in peace and harmony'. Just like we do at
home.

PATTERSON. Oh, Gina, for God's sake –

GINA. And of course you brought me here to make these
people be the kind of people we want them to be. But what
you really meant was: Please, become the kind of people we
want us to be.

TOM. Well, not utterly successfully/ it seems –

KELIMA *is in the darkness, listening.*

GINA. Dead right. And so faced with having our idea of virtue
dumped on them from 15,000 feet, they find a way out
which you can't refuse and surprise surprise it's the second
worst for everyone.

TOM. Now, look. We brought you here to make a peace. Yes,
what we wanted was a multi-ethnic liberal democracy. But

it seems we can't have that and for now the alternative is a bloody civil war. And surely this is preferable to that. Unless anything's that short of everything is of no interest to you.

GINA. 'For now'?

TOM. For now.

GINA. Oh come on Tom. You surely cannot think these people can be ever smart or nice enough to sort this thing out for themselves?

TOM is furious but cannot vent his anger. PATTERSON takes over.

PATTERSON. Hey, you know. There is a story, of a friend of ours. Who was faced with a bad choice – a choice she shouldn't have been faced with – and quite rightly refused to take it. But unfortunately her refusal led to one and maybe two unnecessary deaths. And so she skulks off home to try and wash away her guilt at keeping her hands clean.

Pause. PATTERSON and TOM are aware that KELIMA is there.

You're right. It's not the best deal. But now it's on the table every other option's worse. Not least for the Drozhdan population. So we would be very grateful if you would identify Ms Bejta's reservations and then answer them. As a matter of the utmost urgency.

PATTERSON and TOM go out. GINA sees KELIMA.

GINA. Well?

KELIMA. Well, as they say, the river forms a natural boundary.

GINA. I'm sorry, I don't understand.

KELIMA. So under nice new map, Bazarat, its bridge, its cemetery and its military policemen, all are in Kavkhazia.

Pause.

GINA. Of course.

Pause.

Of course, it's possible, in time, that the Kavkhazians themselves might bring the perpetrators / to justice . . .

KELIMA. Oh, you think so? Those who say that what happen there is prevention of a pogrom? You think they can be ever quite so smart or nice as that?

Pause. She sees ROMAN, *entering and walking down on to the lower deck.*

So tell me. You who say so often, that we acknowledge and confront our past, tell me what shall I say to the mothers of the people who die there? To my mother? When those who kill so many there and elsewhere get off free. What do I say to her?

GINA *is silent.*

ROMAN (*to* KELIMA). You tell her that Miss Olsson is quite right. That we get to keep our monasteries and power stations but we lose our mountains and our nickel and our coal. And you get your country but it's only half a country and the Americans are stuck with our great President and I wager that their pipeline ends up running south through Gezekhstan. And we end up with the second worst for everyone because we are the kind of people that we are.

GINA. You know I don't believe that.

ROMAN. Look. I wanted Finland to succeed. I wanted to make history. But we find there's too much history already. And now we should both go and sign away Miss Olsson's hopes and dreams for us.

KELIMA. Oh yes.

To GINA:

So do I sign?

GINA. You're asking me?

KELIMA. I'm asking you.

Pause.

GINA. You know that I can't answer that. You know it has to be your call.

KELIMA. My call. Of course. For you are Western European.

Slight pause.

GINA. Yes?

KELIMA. You are not American. You read, you study, and you understand. And having understood you do not judge. You listen. You do not impose. But still, you stand above.

GINA *shakes her head.*

I think you cannot stand above. If we dress up our interests as principles, then so do you. But we – we cannot stand below. What is right in USA or Finland is right everywhere. Even in Godforsaken former Soviet Republic. There cannot be one rule for us and one for you. Which mean you cannot stand aside from this. An unjust peace is not always second worst. In fact, in long run, it may be worst of all.

Slight pause.

So Gina Olsson once again I ask you. Tell me what to do. Or please, get out of the affairs of what remain of tourist wonderland Drozhdania, and leave us to the fate that we deserve.

ROMAN *remembers when he last heard those words.*

ROMAN. I beg your pardon?

KELIMA. I'm sorry. You have a problem with my English?

ROMAN. No. I have no problem with your English.

KELIMA. Good.

ROMAN. Miss Bejta, we did not quite make handshake in Geneva. Now we have agreement may we shake hands now?

KELIMA. 'We have agreement'.

ROMAN. Well, if you agree.

KELIMA. Well, that remain yet to be seen.

Suddenly, ROMAN *takes both of* KELIMA*'s hands.*

Uh . . .

ROMAN. Yes.

KELIMA. What's this?

ROMAN. You don't remember.

KELIMA. What should I remember?

ROMAN. 'In the name of God, the compassionate, the merciful'. Chapter 10, verse 92. 'This day shall we save thee in thy body, so that thou might be a sign to those who will come after'.

GINA. What?

ROMAN. A good act. On a little patch of common ground. But that was then, and this is now.

He goes upstairs, meeting TOM PATTERSON, *and* AL, *coming back out and down to* KELIMA, *with a mobile phone.*

GINA. What does he mean?

KELIMA. I've no idea.

TOM. Miss Bejta, there's a call for you.

GINA. What, now?

TOM. Yes, now.

KELIMA. I call back.

PATTERSON. This is not that kind of call.

KELIMA *shrugs, takes the phone.*

KELIMA. Hallo.

Oh, yes. hallo.

Yes, well . . .

Yes, as you say, a compromise. In everybody's best interests. As all best compromises are.

Yes I do very much so hope so. Soon.

She closes the call and hands the phone to PATTERSON.

(*To* TOM.) He speak to everyone?

TOM. He speaks to everyone. And now we're nearly through.

TOM *gestures to the others to go back in.* TOM,
PATTERSON *and* ROMAN *go back up and out.*

KELIMA. It is pathetic. He ask me if I will go home. I lie.

AL. Why aren't you going home?

KELIMA. I ask Ms Olsson what I should say. She has no
answer. I suspect my friends who will receive no justice, I
suspect they have an answer.

Slight pause.

GINA. You let him go.

KELIMA. Then I have a choice. I do not think I have a choice
today.

She goes out.

AL. Who let who go?

GINA. It doesn't matter.

AL. Oh?

Pause.

GINA. Someone did the opposite of what you might expect of
them. Did something better than you might expect of them.
Someone faced with a hard choice, made a brave one.

Slight pause.

Then, not now.

*Behind them, television screens come on. Virtual reality,
three-dimensional images of the country seen from an airplane, manipulable in three dimensions. Silhouetted against
the images are* AL, HASIM, ROMAN, PATTERSON,
TOM, YURI VASILEVICH, ZELIM, EMELA. *Gradually,
as the* MEN *negotiate, the light from the televisions fades.*

HASIM. No, that's Kudjali. It's a Muslim village.

ROMAN. Well, predominantly. As is Ferazi.

EMELA (*Drozhdani, to* ZELIM). Kudjaali Müselmandır.
[Kudjali's Muslim.]

AL. And that's Sestri Brod?

HASIM. Yours.

ROMAN. Abandoned. Can we find the military highway?

YURI VASILEVICH. Left three degrees.

HASIM. Sumgat. Mixed.

ZELIM (*Drozhdani, to* EMELA). Bela chayı mı o? [Is that the Bela river?]

AL. Shouldn't the highway be the border here?

EMELA. Commander Zagayev asks, is that the Bela River?

ROMAN. Yes.

HASIM. The problem is you see the military highway at this point is not defensible.

EMELA (*Drozhdani, to* ZELIM). Müdafia edilmes. [Undefensible.]

HASIM. You see, you can attack it from the ridge.

EMELA (*Drozhdani, to* ZELIM). Onu hamla edabilirsan. [You can attack it.]

ROMAN. For us we need the other villages.

AL. Is that a road along the ridge?

EMELA (*Drozhdani, to* ZELIM). Yol var. [The road.]

ZELIM (*Drozhdani*). Bu asfalt edilmamish bir yol. [It's an unpaved track.]

PATTERSON. What kind of road is it?

EMELA. The Commander says it's just a track. It isn't even paved.

TOM. Easy. We'll pave it.

HASIM. That is our bridge.

EMELA (*Drozhdani, to* ZELIM). Asfalt ettirajaqlar onu. [They will pave it.]

AL. That's a monastery.

HASIM. Across the river from a mosque.

EMELA (*Drozhdani, to* ZELIM). O masjiddir. [That's a
mosque.]

YURI VASILEVICH. Then you blow the bridge and the river
is the frontier.

ROMAN. You can't.

EMELA (*Drozhdani, to* ZELIM). Körpüyü partlatamaslar.
[They can't blow up the bridge.]

YURI VASILEVICH. Why not?

ROMAN. You need it for the road.

Darkness.

Scene Five

*Two years later. A hall in Drozhdania. It's threadbare and
cold, and currently in darkness.* FLOSS *is leading a session
with a group of young people. She comes forward carrying a
table and a torch.* ASLAN, *a 12-year-old Drozhdan boy,
brings a plastic chair, a black rubbish bag of objects and an
oil lamp.* FLOSS *puts down the table,* ASLAN *puts the chair
down beside it and lights the lamp. There's an edgy, slightly
threatened atmosphere from the beginning.*

FLOSS. Look, I'm so sorry. Petrol. Shall we make a start?

ASLAN (*translates into Drozhdani*). Bashlarıkh. [Let's begin.]

ASLAN *takes the objects out of the bag and places them on
the table. They are seemingly random, mostly domestic
objects: mugs, photographs, postcards, shoes, magazines
and newspapers, a kite, tools, an empty but elaborately
shaped duty free whisky bottle. Once* ASLAN *has started,
a door opens and shuts.* FLOSS *carries on anyway.*

FLOSS. Well, hi. Good evening. Now you'll remember last week we did the silent tableaux. To start us off, could somebody describe what happened in one of them?

ASLAN (*translates into Drozhdani*). Istayir ki kimsa insan haykallardan biri tasvir etsa. [She wants someone to describe one of the human sculptures.]

FLOSS. I thought the family one was particularly interesting.

ASLAN (*translates into Drozhdani*). Balka aila tablosu. [Maybe the family one.]

FLOSS. It was done three ways. In the first . . .

The lights come on. The fittings are very primitive.

Aha. The government must have paid the bill.

Lights flicker.

Or at least put something on account.

ASLAN (*translates into Drozhdani*). Hökumat balka hesaabın bahzısı ödadi. [The government might have paid some of the bill.]

Hardly any laughter. She notices people she didn't expect to see.

FLOSS. Oh, right. I see.

Pause.

FLOSS. Well. Today I want to start with these. These are things I asked you to bring in, things that are significant to you. First, this is a woman's weekly magazine. It's German but it could be any language. It's the kind of thing that in the west you read and throw away. I wonder why it's so important to the person who brought it here.

ASLAN (*translates into Drozhdani*). Bu zhurnal niya mühüm? [Why is this magazine important?]

FLOSS *waits for a response. None comes. She carries on.*

FLOSS. I wonder . . . is the sandal, does it belong to a baby of a person here?

ASLAN (*translates into Drozhdani*). Ushaq tuflısı haqqında sorushur kime aaitti filan. [She is wondering about the child's shoe and who it might have belonged to]

No reply. FLOSS *picks up a kite.*

FLOSS. And here a kite. I heard that they were banning kites. Along with audio cassettes and televisions and women in employment.

ASLAN *looks at her; she shakes her head.*

This is of course impossible. With these men here.

She shakes her head to ASLAN; *he needn't translate. A bearded* PARAMILITARY *with a green headband walks from the audience on to the stage.*

But for what it's worth, the main thing I had planned to do today was to explore the situation of a small village school which in the war was run by, by the people who ran things at home, while the men were all away. And then a hero comes back from the war . . .

PARAMILITARY. Yes I think you know that this is not a good idea.

Pause.

FLOSS. Well, it's not a good idea with all your people standing round.

PARAMILITARY. 'Your people'. Where you come from?

FLOSS. London. So are you Drozhdanian?

PARAMILITARY. No. I am from Kabul. But I have been fighting for my cousins here.

FLOSS. Fighting for what?

PARAMILITARY. For an independent country which has made its choice.

FLOSS. Oh, you think so?

PARAMILITARY. As opposed yes to the choices you imposed on them. Colonialism, Marxism. And now global market place.

FLOSS. I hear you.

Another PARAMILITARY *walks on to the stage.*

2nd PARAMILITARY (*Drozhdani*). Onu khaarija tulla!
[Throw her out.]

PARAMILITARY. He thinks that you should leave.

FLOSS. Here? Or the country.

2nd PARAMILITARY (*Drozhdani*). Kifaayettir. [She's done
enough.]

PARAMILITARY. He thinks you've done enough.

FLOSS. I hear him too.

She turns out front, speaking to the group.

I have abandoned people here before. I do not intend to
abandon them again.

ASLAN *looks questioningly. She shakes her head.*

These people want to stop the meetings. But I don't think
it's their call.

She nods at ASLAN *to translate that.*

ASLAN (*translates into Drozhdani*). Askar, görüshü
sakhlamaq istayirlar. O deyir ki hakları yokh. [The soldiers
want to stop the meetings. She says it isn't their decision.]

FLOSS. So I'm going to take a vote.

ASLAN (*translates into Drozhdani*). Sas verma istayir. [She's
going to take a vote.]

2nd PARAMILITARY (*Drozhdani*). Onlara sas mi verdirir?
[She's going to have them *vote*?]

PARAMILITARY. You know, I think they understand that it
would not be well advised to raise their hands.

FLOSS. OK. Good point. So me must find another way. I
know . . . let's say that some of you are liars. Some of you
tell truth. But only you know which you are.

ASLAN (*translates into Drozhdani*). Bahzımız yalanja, bahzımız haqiqat derik. [Some of us are liars. Some of us tell truth.]

FLOSS. Now translate this carefully. If I ask you to put up your hands if you want me to obey these men, what would you do?

The PARAMILITARIES *look at each other.*

Tell them.

ASLAN (*translates into Drozhdani*). Agar sizdan rijaa eder ki: alinizi qaldırın agar siz onun bu kishilari itaat etmasini isteyarsanız, na edajaqsiniz? [If she asks you to put up your hands if you want her to obey these men, what would you do?]

Silence as FLOSS, ASLAN *and the* PARAMILITARIES *watch.*

2nd PARAMILITARY. Na deyirlar? [What are they saying?]

1st PARAMILITARY (*to* FLOSS). What do they say?

FLOSS. You heard.

End of play.

Afterword

The Prisoner's Dilemma is the third of what has turned out to
be a loosely-connected series of plays about the aftermath of
the fall of the Berlin Wall. Now that event has become part of
history it seems – like the French Revolution and the outcome
of the Second World War – to have been inevitable. In fact,
it was a huge surprise. As cold warriors argued, one of the
particular iniquities of totalitarian communism was that it had
proved so durable.

In the first play (*The Shape of the Table*, 1990) I tried to
imagine what it's like to emerge from forty years of political
failure into a new world. Premiered a day before the first
anniversary of the fall of the Wall, the play was set before and
during the actual moment of revolution in a generic East
European country, and contrasted the hopes of the victors with
the sense of regret and loss among the vanquished. The second
play (*Pentecost*, 1994–5) was about the limitations of the new
world order – how for all its universal pretensions the idea of
'Europe' was in practice limited politically, culturally,
economically and physically. As a character put it, as soon as
the walls between Eastern Europe and the west came down,
new walls were erected just as high the other side.

The Shape of the Table was set in central Europe, and
Pentecost a little further east, in the contested zone between
Catholicism and the Orthodox world. *The Prisoner's Dilemma*
is set on Europe's outer edge, where the Orthodox world faces
Islam. Inspired by Jane Corbin's television documentary on the
Oslo peace process, the play is about attempts to settle two
kinds of conflict, those which emerged in the wake of the Cold
War and those long-standing conflicts which had appeared
intractable but which after 1989 seemed open to resolution.

In addition to their importance, these conflicts were richly
dramatic, in a way that earlier twentieth-century conflicts were
not. In both world wars, commanders in their capitals moved

conscript armies across largely distant battlefields (Hitler and
Stalin never met). In the Cold War, personal contacts between
the contending superpowers were largely limited to ceremonial
summitry. However, after the wall came down, a much more
personal kind of warfare emerged. Just before the Bosnian war
broke out, the speaker of the Bosnian legislature and the leader
of the Bosnian Muslims met in the now abandoned parliament
building for secret talks at night. Once parliamentary colleagues,
now competing warlords armed with machine guns, Momcilo
Krajisnik insisted to Alija Izetbegovic that there was no
alternative to the forced partition of multi-ethnic Sarajevo.
Joking about the superiority of his weaponry, Krajisnik gave
Izetbegovic the parting gift of a pen. Now one is president of
his country and the other on trial for war crimes.

The conflicts that emerged in the wake of the Cold War are full
of such poignant confrontations between colleagues turned
combatants (in 1990, Izetbegovic and Radovan Karadzic stood
on a bridge over the Drina river, commemorating the Yugoslav
war dead and pledging that 'blood must never flow down the
Drina river ever again'). This is true too of the seemingly
intractable conflicts – South Africa, Northern Ireland, the
Middle East – which suddenly seemed soluble when the Cold
War was over. Here, it was not so much friends turning into
foes as the other way round, as secret mediators sought to
persuade guerrilla leaders and beleagured governments to get
up close and personal. In the secret Norwegian peace
negotiations, Israeli and Palestinian politicians were spirited
from the cauldron of the middle east into the private homes
of Norwegian diplomats, to eat fine food, contemplate the
mountain scenery, play with their hosts' children and negotiate
the Oslo agreement. Flying together in government planes,
ANC and Nationalist Party leaders bonded in remote game
lodges in the South African bush. In Northern Ireland,
decommissioning overseer General John de Chastelain shares
a passion for fly fishing with Martin McGuinness of Sinn Fein.

In practice richly dramatic, the theory of peacemaking too is
dominated by the language of play-making. Academics,
diplomats, soldiers and politicians use sophisticated roleplay
models to prepare for actual negotiations as well as to explore

contemporary, historical and invented conflicts. Historians use roleplay to analyse the moves and counter moves of key Cold War moments at Crisis Revisited conferences. American diplomats encourage South American governments to role-play negotiations with guerrilla insurgents. In one American university roleplay, undertaken as the Kosovo war was joined, the Serb position was being put by a Russian diplomat who walked out of the roleplay in protest at NATO's actions. Students in Bradford University's department of peace studies simulate relief convoys trying to get past belligerent Serbs played by Royal Military Policemen on the North Yorkshire moors. As President Martti Ahtisaari of Finland, Strobe Talbott of the US state department and Russia's Viktor Chermonyrdin drew up the deal that would end the NATO bombing of Kosovo in Stalin's dacha outside Moscow, Chermonyrdin insisted that a fourth chair be placed at the table, representing President Milosevic and thus mutely insisting that they see their proposals through his eyes.

In addition, games like Chicken and indeed Prisoner's Dilemma have proved remarkably helpful in thinking about international conflict, and where they've proved wanting, there are theorists on hand to build on and improve them. For example, a dissident game theorist called Nigel Howard has developed a paradigm of negotiation actually called dramatheory. In a model which has influenced NATO thinking on peacemaking, Howard argues that emotion (and thus 'irrationality') is not only inevitable but vital in negotiations. Sooner or later, negotiators must confront the intractable contradictions of their and their opponents' positions (from 'can you believe that I will do the thing I'm threatening to do?' all the way to 'do I trust you to carry out any agreement?'). It is at this 'moment of truth' that emotion forces the parties to reconstitute their positions in such a way that threats become realistic and trust can be gained. It is a theoretical explanation of the platitude that a good row often clears the air; as in the incident – memorably described by Jane Corbin – in which the chief Palestinian negotiator stalked out of a vital meeting, provoking his Israeli opponent to announce that this proved they'd strike their deal today (as indeed they did).

When I began thinking about how to use such metaphors to create a representative post-Cold War conflict, it seemed that I was dramatising a success story. By the end of the 90s, things looked different. Following the unqualified success of negotiations in South Africa and what appeared to be breakthroughs in the Middle East and Northern Ireland, peace settlements were beginning to unravel. The Northern Ireland process appeared to grind to a halt. The techniques which had ended the Bosnian war at Dayton failed to resolve the Kosovo conflict at Rambouillet. Despite or maybe even because of the success of Oslo, the Middle East settlement crumbled and the intifada exploded once again. As a consequence, the confidence of governments in conflict resolution wavered and suddenly it was the peacemakers themselves whose strategies, techniques and motivation were called into question. Whether acquiescing in the ill-gotten gains of bandit armies or seeking to impose quick-fix western solutions, both European and American peacemakers faced charges that far from being honest brokers they had their own agendas, which were not always in the interests of the people they were claiming to help. Finally, surely, the era of hope for a new kind of peace-making, which began with the fall of the Berlin Wall on 9 November 1989, was brought to an end by the events of 11 September 2001.

This is so in three obvious respects. First, and most importantly, the 11 September attackers were neither conducting nor seeking to conduct negotiations towards any kind of settlement. Second, in this conflict, the United States is not a peacemaker but a combatant, whose interest in the outcome is neither disputed nor concealed. Third, there is the question of scale. Without seeking to diminish the suffering of victims of terrorism over the last thirty years, 11 September dwarfs any other man-made carnage outside of a warzone. Yes, the American death toll was substantially less than those who were murdered in two days at Srebrenica. But, still, more people died in a couple of hours on 11 September than have died in thirty years of the troubles in Northern Ireland. It is certainly the biggest single event in the world since the collapse of communism.

But all of that said, not everything has changed. Conventional, post-Cold War conflicts will go on, as will negotiations to resolve them. It would be optimistic to think that wars in Macedonia and Chechnya are over, and naive to think that the United States will abandon its interest in Caspian oil, and thus in resolving the dispute between Armenia and Azerbaijan. Even in Afghanistan, the processes have grown more recognisable: following Oslo, Dayton and Rambouillet, another group of mutually suspicious parties is whisked off into a culturally alien environment (in this case, a luxury hilltop hotel outside Bonn) to try and negotiate a durable political deal (while the World Bank hosts parallel discussions in Pakistan about how the west can use its economic clout to reconstruct Afghanistan in its own image).

Finally, the fact that the attackers were not negotiating doesn't mean that a conversation wasn't taking place. People have argued that the whole language of game-theory is inappropriate to the current conflict: the suicide bomber is clearly not interested in playing Prisoner's Dilemma, and by definition has misunderstood the rules of Chicken. But it is vital that peacemakers as well as warmongers understand how the world looks from the point of view of those from whom Al Qaida recruits, and it is the essence of both Chicken and Prisoner's Dilemma that it requires players to see the world through other eyes. In Prisoner's Dilemma, if you do what seems best for you (whatever the other guy decides) your best option is to rat. However, if you do what's best for the other guy – miraculously – you both end up better off. The risk is – as a character puts it in my play – that you have to rely on the other guy being smart enough or nice enough to work that out.

Drama's power has always been that it invites – indeed, requires – the audience to empathise. Without the comforting security of the narrative voice (whether author or central character), the dramatist has to invite the audience to see the world he creates from competing perspectives. As Wilde said, you put a man in a mask and he will tell you the truth. The turning point in a game of Prisoner's Dilemma comes not when you work out what the other person's thinking, but when you work out that the other person is trying to do the same.

Conflict resolution's age of innocence is over, and military force may well resolve the current conflict in the short term. But a final settlement will rely on people understanding each other and changing their behaviour as a result. The events of late 2001 will look no less enormous, but they may look more familiar.

David Edgar
December 2001

This is a revised and extended version of a piece first published in The Guardian *on 7 July 2001.*

War and Peace after the Cold War: a Selective Chronology

1989   *November:* Breaching of the Berlin Wall leads to the
fall of communist governments in Eastern Europe.

1990   Secret talks between IRA and former MI6 officer.
February: Nelson Mandela released from prison.
August: Failed coup by Communist hard-liners against
Mikhail Gorbachev. ANC suspends its armed struggle
in South Africa.
November: Chechnya Congress declares Chechnya
independent.
December: Break up of Soviet Union.

1991   *January-February:* America and its allies win the Gulf
war against Iraq.
June: Slovenia secedes from Yugoslavia.
October: John Hume begins his initiative to end the
war in Northern Ireland.
November: Serbia takes Vukovar in eastern Croatia.
December: Negotiations for majority rule begin in
South Africa. The European Union recognises
independent Croatia.

1992   *March:* Bosnia declares itself independent and Bosnian
war begins.
June: Gerry Adams joins John Hume in drafting
document for peace in Northern Ireland.
June: Nelson Mandela breaks off South African peace
talks after 48 people are killed in township attack.
August: Torture and starvation of Muslim prisoners at
Omarska concentration camp in northern Bosnia exposed.
December: ANC conducts private negotiations with
Nationalist government in the South African bush.

1993 *January:* Negotiations in Geneva on Vance/Owen plan to end Bosnian war. Secret talks between Palestinians and Israelis begin in Norway.
March: Face-to-face meetings between British government representatives and Sinn Fein.
September: Yitzak Rabin and Yasser Arafat sign the Oslo agreement in Washington.
December: British and Irish governments make Downing Street Declaration on the future of Northern Ireland.

1994 *January:* Muslim/Croat war breaks out in Bosnia.
April: ANC wins South Africa's first free elections and Nelson Mandela becomes President.
September: IRA ceasefire in Northern Ireland.
December: Russian troops attack the Chechen capital Grozny.

1995 *July:* Up to 8,000 Muslims massacred by Serb forces after the fall of Srebrenica.
August: Shelling of Sarajevo market place kills 37 and leads to NATO bombing of Serbian positions.
November: Peace talks at Dayton, Ohio, settle the conflict in Bosnia.

1996 *February:* Palestinian suicide bombers kill 54 people and threaten peace process.
August: Peace deal in Chechnya leads to Russian withdrawal.

1998 *April:* Good Friday agreement in Northern Ireland.

1999 *January:* Serb paramilitaries kill 45 ethnic Albanians in Racak, Kosovo.
February: Proximity talks to avert war in Kosovo begin at Rambouillet in France.
March: Following the failure of the Rambouillet negotiations, NATO begins its bombing campaign against Serbia, leading to mass ethnic cleansing of the Albanian population of Kosovo.
June: NATO ends its bombing campaign as Serbs prepare to leave Kosovo and UN troops move in.

July: 13 Serb farmers are massacred in Graco, Kosovo.
October: Russian troops mount second invasion of
breakaway Chechen republic.
November: Power-sharing executive formed in
Northern Ireland.

2000   *February:* Power-sharing executive suspended in
Northern Ireland.
May: Power-sharing executive restored in Northern
Ireland.
September: Ariel Sharon's visit to the Dome on the
Rock in Jerusalem provokes renewed violence in Israel
and Palestine.
November: Slobodan Milosevic loses Yugoslav
Presidential election and is overthrown.

2001   *January:* Palestinians reject US-brokered peace deal in
the dying days of the Clinton Presidency as middle east
conflict continues.
June: Slobodan Milosevic is extradited to the Hague to
face war crimes charges.
August: NATO troops enter Macedonia to police peace
deal between the government and ethnic Albanian rebels.
September: Terrorists kill up to 5,000 in New York and
Washington.
October: The IRA begins decommissioning its weapons.
November: After a month of American bombing, the
Taliban surrender Kabul to the Northern Alliance and
negotiations for a new government of Afghanistan
begin.